Don't Wear a Cowboy Hat
Unless You are a Cowboy

And Other Grumblings
from a Cranky Curmudgeon

by Robert W. Bly

"It turns out that helping is the main thing. If you feel that you have a use, if you think your writing furthers life or truth in some way, then you keep writing. But if that feeling stops, you have to find something else to do."

–Nicholas Baker, *The Anthologist*
(Simon & Schuster, 2009), p. 54.

Praise for Bob Bly

"If you asked me who the number one 'sell yourself' master in the world is, I'd have to say it is, without question, Bob Bly."

—Michael Masterson

"You are awesome! I will always come to you first for the products that I need. You have class, integrity, brilliance, are naturally gifted, and second to none! I am impressed with and appreciate your prompt response."

—Adella Pugh

"Once in a blue moon, you get the chance to meet a living legend, one of the great men who shaped his chosen field. In my unending pursuit of powerful marketing, I came face-to-face with just such a man. Robert Bly is America's Top Copywriter and a genius marketer. He's authored over 70 books for McGraw-Hill and others, and gets paid more per word than nearly every author in America. Like all great men, he is a teacher and mentor extraordinaire. He freely shares the secrets of turning marketing into money."

—Dick Larkin

"The best writing teacher in the business!"

–Tom Peric

"Bob, your stuff is always so good that even though I'm retired now, I have to read it!"

–Gary Bencivenga

"You are someone I've grown to admire greatly. You share your knowledge with and encourage people in achieving their dreams, trying new things, and learning tricks of the trade. It's a rare 'guru' in our world today who is thoughtful and kind enough to help up-and-comers find the path to success. In my opinion, you are the very best. I'm grateful to you."

–Linda Capriotti

"During the past 20 years, Bob Bly has become one of America's leading direct response copywriters. He has probably done more to teach other writers the craft of effective and persuasive writing than anyone else."

–Roger C. Parker

"After considering a number of high-level marketing professionals and reflecting on the matter for several weeks, I made the decision to ask Bob Bly to share the stage with me for my Twin Keys to Wealth-Building Conference. The reason I chose Bob is because I am convinced that he can deliver more tangible value to conference attendees than any other marketing or Internet expert on the planet."

—Robert Ringer, best-selling author

"I love your e-mails. Read every single one of them as they come in."

—Dr. Paul Hartunian

"I have huge admiration for your work. You're one of the few guys out there selling real information—and selling it at a reasonable price! I think what you're doing is head and shoulders above others."

—Mark Joyner

"I receive so many e-mail offers—too many—but Bob always delivers a product worth having. The marketplace for writing and marketing products has become over-hyped; in that environment it's reaffirming to see that Bob continues to stand for a level of quality that matters—and happily, at a price that works."

—Peg Prideaux

"Watch Bob Bly very closely. He's a very intelligent marketer who knows how to get results and bring in the money!"

—John Kidd

"I have enjoyed all of the books that I have read of yours. I appreciate your no-nonsense, take-it-to-the-bank advice that you deliver."

—Nicholas J. Loise, RSVP Chicago

"The Handbook and your bonus are first class. I'm very pleased. You never disappoint."

—Louis J. Wasser, Copywriter

"The product promos you've been sending have plenty of content. I look forward to your e-mails, because they are great idea generators. And your price points are very reasonable. I'd rather pay from $29-$97 for one of your products than the $299-$500 I've been dishing out to others. Your current business model is brilliant and fair."

–Stanley M. Jackson

"I am delighted every time I take one of your recommendations! You haven't steered me wrong once, and each of your products has been well worth every penny invested."

–Pat Johnson

"I learn a lot from your e-mails even when they point to other products or products you sell. I like learning. Keep it coming."

–Pat McKenzie

"Yours are one of the e-mails that I do enjoy and I order from you as often as I think I can use the help."

–Joe Alagna

"I eagerly anticipate your e-mails–all of them. I've made several purchases. You offer a lot of great advice and insight free. You offer a lot of [other] great advice and insight at very reasonable prices, typically with immediate delivery. Personally, I wouldn't want to miss the opportunity to consider anything you think might be helpful."

–Linda Byam

"You develop a helpful product, describe it in detail, make it easy to access online, post a reasonable price and offer a money-back guarantee. Personally, I thank you for your contribution. I've purchased many of your products. And I've made returns. You stand by what you sell, plus."

–Lynn Roberts

"What we receive free from you and others has the potential to ignite countless ideas–priceless ones on occasion. The opportunity to in turn purchase something from the 'sales' e-mails is complementary to you sharing so much priceless info with us–your willing subscribers. Press on and keep allowing us to benefit from your years of experience however you share it."

–Eddie Stephen

Acknowledgments

Thanks to those subscribers to my e-newsletter The Direct Response Letter who asked me questions and suggested topics that sparked the essays in these chapters.

To the memory of
Leslie Howard

Table of Contents

Introduction

For years, I've published a twice-weekly e-newsletter that goes to about 65,000 subscribers.

Originally I dispensed strictly marketing advice. But then I broadened the scope to encompass more areas of business success and life in general.

Then a problem arose: as I get older, I get crankier and more irritable. I hold to the belief that older people as a rule are correct more often than younger people, because, as my favorite comic Louis CK has observed, their opinions are based on more information.

This increasingly grouchy and cynical attitude began to assert itself in my online essays, which I feared would alienate my subscribers. More and more of my essays became what is known in information marketing as "rants"–complains against the stupidity of the status quo.

But to my great surprise, my subscribers loved these rants and opinionated ramblings–and the more personal they were, the better they loved them.

Once I realized that, I continued to indulge myself. And today, my e-newsletter is probably a 70/30 mixture of personal opinions on important business and life topics vs. straightforward tips on marketing topics.

Is this the best advice in the world on business and life? Probably not, but it is the best I can give you, based on my experience as a marketer, entrepreneur, and writer since 1979. You can read my bio at the back of the book, along with testimonials from my e-newsletter subscribers, to determine whether I am worth listening to.

I continue to write and distribute the essays online, so if you have a question, e-mail it to me and I may, if I feel qualified and able, answer it in a future issue: rwbly@bly.com

In addition, you can get all my future e-mail essays free by signing up for my e-newsletter here: www.bly.com/reports. When you sign up, you also get 4 free bonus reports totaling 200 pages with a retail value of over $100. Details are on the sign-up page.

It's my hope that by reading this book, you will in plain and easy-to-read language get advice and ideas that can help you:

- Make and save more money.
- Have greater freedom and control of your life.
- Enjoy meaningful work that you absolutely love.
- Improve your business and personal relationships.
- Become financially secure.
- Do what you want and avoid doing things you don't want to do.

I sincerely believe that even if you only get one good idea for improving just one of the areas named above, it will pay back the modest cost of this book tenfold or more–not a bad return on your reading investment.

1

The Law of Attraction is Baloney

Self-help gurus and motivational speakers love to tell us that whatever we want, we can do, have, or become.

Napoleon Hill said, "Whatever the mind can conceive and believe, it can achieve."

Earl Nightingale: "Whatever we plant in our subconscious mind and nourish with repetition and emotion will one day become a reality."

The problem with this is: it's often not true.

Examples:

** Unless you have a high IQ, you can't become an astrophysicist.

** Unless you are athletic, you won't get drafted by the Patriots.

** Unless you can sing, you probably won't win American Idol and get a record deal.

** Unless you're strong and can fight, you probably can't KO Lennox Lewis.

What many positive thinkers ignore is that it takes more than just positive thoughts to achieve a goal.

And here's what it does take to do or become what you desire:

>> First, you need the equipment: the aptitude, affinity, and knack for a particular field or profession.

Example: I am 56, short, dumpy, and nonathletic. I would like to be the Giants quarterback. But no matter what I think, it isn't going to happen, even if Manning continues to have a terrible season.

But I do have an affinity for teaching. So I have routinely been paid thousands of dollars a day to give training classes and seminars.

>> Second, you need desire.

This is especially true in fields like acting, music, and sports where competition for a limited number of opportunities is incredibly fierce.

Unless you have a burning desire for the goal, you won't stick with it and make the effort it takes to get there.

>> Third, you must be persistent.

The old adage: If at first you don't succeed, try, try again.

Winston Churchill: "Never give up."

In my observation, most people who want to pursue an accomplishment or achievement give up way too early.

>> Fourth, talent.

You should have some natural talent or, if not, enormous enthusiasm for the field in which you want to make your mark.

If you are not naturally talented, you can develop many of the skills you need (e.g. Website design) through practice and study.

>> Fifth, skill.

In today's competitive world, it's tough to make a go of things if you are poor or mediocre in your profession.

To increase the odds of success in your favor, you must get really good at what you do. The key is: practice.

Mark Ford says you can get good at just about anything by doing it for a thousand hours...and become a master when you have done it for ten thousand hours.

>> Sixth, training.

Your training may be on the job or in the classroom. It could be night school, seminars, in-house courses offered by your company, or college.

But you must acquire the basic knowledge practitioners in your field are expected to have.

As a copywriter since 1979, I knew how to write.

But when SEO become a discipline some years ago, I took an expensive Direct Marketing Association self-study course to learn it.

>> Seventh, you need connections.

Very few people realize their dreams entirely on their own.

Cultivating a network of colleagues, specialists, and potential clients or employers can give you an enviable shortcut to your goal.

By the way, if you do read one author who writes about success, I recommend Brian Tracy.

2

Those Who Can, Teach

If you believe, as so many do, that "those who can, do; those who can't, teach"—get it out of your head now.

The fact is that those at the top of their profession are often the most active not only as practitioners but also as both students and teachers.

The last time I wrote about this, I received a huge amount of e-mail from my subscribers and Facebook friends.

They overwhelmingly agreed that: (a) the "those who can't, teach" adage is absurd and (b) teaching others what you know is an integral and important activity for most professions.

Here's just a sampling...

WB: "If nobody who knew what they were doing showed others how it's done, then the only way to learn would be by trial and error or from those who have never been a success at it."

BW: "Teaching is my greatest joy. I love to learn about a wide range of subjects. When I share what I've learned, as do you, I learn even more. Plus, I form new bonds with those I teach, whether in an informal way or in a well-organized workshop. It's all about widening one's perspective and personal growth."

BM: "I've had several careers and taught how-to courses and seminars in all of them. I think it made me a better doer, and it enhanced my business credibility and income."

DG: "As consulting engineers we teach what we do, and we make good money at it. In fact, it set both of us up for retirement some years ago. At this point in my career, I actually enjoy the teaching more than the consulting. Nothing like seeing someone 'get it.'"

JG: "We teach what we wish to learn."

ES: "And we learn best what we choose to teach."

LW: "I have a strong background in the arts. Many very successful musicians in classical music and jazz have enjoyed the psychological effects of teaching and watching novices develop. I could go on and on naming them: violinist Isaac Stern, jazz pianist Hank Jones.

"A few years back I helped edit and rewrite a biography of a famous British classical pianist, Ruth Nye, who is now a very famous teacher. The principal theme of her biographer's book was that Ruth herself studied with one of the greatest pianists of the 20th Century, Claudio Arrau, who himself was also widely known as a great teacher.

"This is true in all the arts. Dutch painter Peter Lastman was famous for his own work, but also for being Rembrandt's teacher. Hollywood is rife with examples of actors who taught other actors (ever listen to the many thank-yous in an Oscar acceptance speech?).

"It's true in sports too. I have cousins in professional baseball and football management who talk about examples of apprenticeships all the time. In our own business, Clayton Makepeace is a glorious example of a man who has made fabulous money as a copywriter and as a man who has derived joy (and financial recompense) for being a great teacher."

My own experience: every time I teach a class, which I did for years at New York University and The Learning Annex, I feel I have learned even more than the students—and my students tell me they have learned a lot.

It always saddens me when I meet someone who thinks both teaching and learning are beyond them.

Many years ago, at a writer's conference, I sat next to a fellow attendee. We were both perusing the conference brochure, selecting the breakout sessions we would go to.

I noticed they had a session on selling a nonfiction book to a major publishing house, and to make conversation, I mentioned to her that it interested me.

She turned up her nose and said haughtily, "That might be good if you are a beginner, but I have already published two books."

I said nothing and smiled. Back then, I had written only 50 books...and I was eagerly looking forward to attending the session to see what tips I could pick up. I guess they worked, because I have written over 30 more books since then.

As my colleague seminar leader Paul Karasik often says to me, "School is never out for the pro"–and that's true whether it means being a student or a teacher.

3

Why Mad Men-Style Advertising is Moronic

For decades there has been an ongoing debate between general advertisers and direct marketers concerning the notion of creativity as essential to good advertising.

Some of my subscribers find this a stimulating discussion, while others have told me they think it has been discussed into oblivion.

But my interest in it was rekindled by a comment Aileen Kelly made in a letter-to-the-editor published in the 9/26/13 issue of the New York Review of Books.

She wrote: "Being original is no protection against being wrong."

The school of general advertisers who value creativity seem to deliberately strive to achieve it in their work, believing that being creative is the only way to make your ads stand out and get noticed.

What these practitioners do not realize is that most advertisements do not work. Some veteran practitioners estimate the success rate of new promotions to vary between 10% and 25%.

Therefore, if your advertisement is a creative breakthrough, it may be a winner because of its originality. But that same originality could also result in a flop, because the ad is based on an untested and unproven idea.

Most direct marketers I know value creativity, but they value testing even higher: we assiduously study what is working, then model our new efforts after these tried and prove promotions as much as we can.

The reason is that if we build on what has already been proven, our success rates can be toward the higher end of the scale—and our flops few and far between.

Let me share with you a cautionary tale...

A major publisher of reference works in the health care field had a marketing director, BC, who was a genuine direct response pro. All his new campaigns, some of which I wrote, were carefully built based upon analysis of previous campaigns.

We would meet every 6 months, lay out all the recent mailings on a conference table, and write the response rate on the outer panel with a bold black marker. Then we would look for common factors shared by the top performers.

Using this methodology, I wrote a mailing for him that outperformed the control 3 to 1:

http://www.bly.com/newsite/Pages/idm.htm

Anyway, my client moved on and was replaced by a less wise marketing director, RB.

RB hired a "creative" Madison Avenue agency that assured him their creativity would produce results far superior to the old "boring" DM I had written.

They convinced him to suspend the customary split testing of the old vs. the new model and spend every marketing dollar on their "creative" mailings.

I think you can guess the result: Madison Avenue's direct mail was a horrific failure. Sales of the product plummeted. Revenues tanked.

It was so bad that RB was summarily fired. Management told him to clean out his office that very day, and security escorted him from the building.

Of course, the creative ad agency probably didn't care much. They had "creative" samples to boast about at the ad shows. And even though their work stank up the joint, they still collected their big ad agency fee, which dwarfed what I had been paid by the same client to triple their sales.

"Great old copy is often better than untested new copy," writes Denny Hatch in his book "The Secrets of Emotional, Hot-Button Copywriting," published by Direct Marketing IQ.

4

How to Respond to Idiots.

One of the drawbacks to being an info marketer is being subjected to the occasional uninformed, just plain ignorant opinion of that rarest of beings: a stupid subscriber.

LB is that rarity. In a recent e-mail, here's her response to me using the term "expensive experience" to describe the hard-won knowledge I share with my subscribers:

"You used the word 'expensive' to describe your experience. That tells me that your primary motive is not to 'share' your experience; it is to 'sell' your experience. You see it as a commodity.

"If sharing were your primary purpose then you would not be concerned with people asking for refunds because at least you would have shared your experience with them.

"This is not a personal attack; I am trying to ascertain whether you truly understand what's going on in your mind, because perhaps you don't honestly know. You may think your primary motive is to share your experience, when actually it is not."

I immediately replied:

"You have made a judgment on my motivation that is totally wrong. Sharing IS my primary motivation for being a writer.

"The two reasons I charge for my information are: (1) I think, like any professional (e.g., doctor, lawyer), I deserve to be compensated for what I know, but more important (2) people do not value what they get for free.

"'Expensive experience' is a Dan Kennedy term. It means our practical knowledge is gained at a great cost in time and money. It does not mean what you say above. I don't just THINK my motivation is sharing. I know it is."

I was tempted to ask LB which school she received her degree in psychology from, and I should have. The point: Consider your qualifications to render the opinions, especially the unsolicited opinions, you deliver to others. If you don't have any, perhaps you are better off remaining silent—or at least raising a question rather than stating your subjective judgment as if it were fact cast in concrete.

Then I noticed her e-mail had no signature file, which meant she was not revealing to me her mailing address or phone number. And so I continued:

"Notice one other difference between our e-mails. Mine has a sig file with my phone number. Yours does not. That means any reader can pick up the phone, call me, and tell me what they think.

"Without a sig file and phone number, you hide behind the safe barrier of e-mail from having to answer me face to face. How brave you are!"

Okay. I guess I lost it. But I don't regret it. At my advanced age, I do not suffer fools gladly, and when someone gives insult, I have great difficulty letting it pass—and increasingly, I do not.

If there's a lesson here, it's a simple one: when you communicate, be willing to take as good as you get. Hiding behind your e-mail—which you do whenever you send one without a sig file—is, as Sylvester Stallone tells his son in Rocky Balboa, what cowards do. And as Rocky says in the movie, "That ain't you."

But that's not the quite the end of this story…

After I wrote this, I was working at my PC at 5am during one of my frequent bouts with insomnia, and I got this follow-up e-mail from LB:

"I stated quite clearly it was not a personal attack, I was trying to help you understand what your primary motive is and thus get to grips with the issue you have with refunds.

The fact you have taken so much offence tells me I struck a nerve. Truth hurts!"

My blood pressure skyrocketing, I instantly replied:

"Wrong yet again. I take offense, and you struck a nerve, not because what you say is correct, but precisely because it is NOT: ignorance irks me to an admittedly irrational degree. I cannot abide people who render inaccurate opinions as if they were true.

"I do not need nor did I ask for your help understanding my motive, because I DO understand it. As stated, it is the compulsion to share with others what I learn—a common impulse shared by billions.

"And I stand by my statement saying you are cowardly for not having a sig file with a phone number in your e-mail: it allows you to pompously render pronouncements without having to face me directly."

5

The Myth of Outdated Information

You know a pet peeve of mine is the ignorance of folks who believe that any information product older than 3 years is antiquated, obsolete, and irrelevant.

Along those lines, subscriber JK writes:

"I have been following you for a number of years and have purchased some of your products. Most are excellent and I have been happy with them.

"You mentioned returns of materials more than three years old. In most cases if the product is over three years old, I will be disappointed with the vendor and may not purchase from them again.

"Some products are evergreen, such as your copywriting products and self improvement products from Brian Tracy and many others.

"Some products are not evergreen. Most any product on Web development (creating

Websites) is obsolete in a year because of how fast the information changes."

Here's my reply to JK:

"I beg to differ. Yes, any product on social media that is over 3 years old is outdated. But my products on Internet marketing are NOT outdated...because the methodology I use is proven and has been consistent for many years.

"That methodology does not incorporate SEO or social media, so I dispute your contention that those products are outdated."

See, here's what all these "this product is too old" whiners do not understand about Internet marketing:

There are literally dozens of different techniques used in driving and converting traffic in Internet marketing.

Yet, you can build and run a wildly profitable Internet marketing business—mine gives me a 6-figure annual income with me putting in literally just 2-3 hours a week on it—using only a handful of them.

That's what the Internet marketing methodology my products teach does: It produces traffic and converts clicks to sales using only a few proven techniques which do not change much over the years.

It deliberately ignores dozens of other techniques including blogging, SEO, and social media. Why? Because you can't do and know everything. And the simpler an online business is, the easier and less time it takes to run.

I am not saying you should avoid those methods. In fact, I use them for some of my other businesses, and I sell information products on all 3—blogging, SEO, and social media.

But the Internet marketing "system" I use doesn't rely on them. So changes in SEO or social media do not render it obsolete in any way. They are just not relevant.

Here's another irritant with regard to outdated information: if a Website URL in one of my info products no longer works, my buyers roar about it.

Well, we had the same thing in the pre-Internet days with my books: the longer the book was in print, the more likely it was that the addresses and phone numbers in them would be outdated, because the resources moved or went out of business. Yet no one complained or asked for a refund.

I fear I will go to my grave fighting and losing this battle. So I have resigned myself to spending the rest of my life (sigh) continually updating my information products (e-books, audio albums, DVDs) as well as my traditionally published books. These days I am always writing a new edition of one of my nonfiction books.

It never ends, but the shame of it is: it's unnecessary, for the reasons I have stated.

So if you see me in the street, shuffling slowly...a gray, worn out, sad, tired little man, barely able to stand...well–it's your fault!

But I won't hold it against you.

Oh, well–back to the keyboard.

6

Why Every Writer Needs a Second Pair of Eyes

The awkward paragraph below appears in a Kindle e-book of my short stories I published:

"No problem," Van Helsing said, looking them up and down appraisingly. "I'm sure there'll be plenty of goulash for everybody." He looked at them appraisingly. "Though I may need to use a bigger pot."

The flaw, of course, is the repetition of "appraisingly."

What makes this error particularly awful is that I read the story half a dozen times before publishing it.

Yet it wasn't until I sat down to read a copy of the published book that I finally noticed the error.

Worse, my fiction writing teacher read and edited the story before the book was published.

So did the professional proofreader I hired to review the book in galley. And they both missed it, as did I.

My point is: whether you are a fiction writer, nonfiction writer, copywriter, or any other kind of writer, it's a challenge to prevent these kinds of sloppy and obvious errors from slipping in.

Therefore, it's my belief that you should NEVER submit a draft to your publisher, printer, or client without having your copy checked over several times...by you as well as by at least one other person.

In my freelance copywriting business, when I come up with a concept for a new promotion—usually consisting of a few headlines and a lead of a few hundred words—I always run it by IB.

IB is on a monthly retainer to me for the express purposes of being available to review and render an immediate opinion on almost everything I write—not only copy for my clients but blog posts, essays, articles, and e-mails and landing pages for my information marketing business.

I often show my concepts to one or two other trusted associates in addition to IB to be sure that my ideas are on the right track—in other words, that they are compelling, fresh, and engaging.

When I have written the copy, I then show it to JK, my proofreader, who goes through it to catch any typos I may have made.

The benefits of this in-house review process are twofold.

First, it enables me to be confident that I am showing only good work to clients, publishers, and subscribers.

Second, it allows me to submit very clean copy, which in turn gives clients and publishers confidence in the work I give them.

Typos and other errors—such as in my example of repeating "appraisingly" twice in one paragraph—jar readers. Spotting even a minor error can go a long way in ruining their opinion of the rest of the piece. Unfortunate, but that's the way it is.

Very early in my career, my client ZC, to my great surprise, told me he thought my copy for his software brochure was weak.

I read it again and didn't see any problem, so I asked him what was wrong.

"You wrote it too quickly and didn't take any care with the work," he said in an annoyed tone.

I asked ZC how he reached this conclusion.

His answer: "You must have rushed it because on page 3, you misspelled 'anachronism.'"

I don't ever again want to have the client or reader become unfairly prejudiced against a great piece of copy for the sole reason that it contains a sloppy typo.

Neither do you.

7

Are You an "Accessible Expert"?

Reader FL recently tried to get in touch with his favorite Internet marketing teacher...let's call this guru Mr. X...with disappointing results.

"I thought: why not reach out and connect with him?" says FL. "Good luck with that idea–the guy lives behind an electronic fortress...which is odd given the story he tells about accessibility in his book."

The guru in question, Mr. X, a guy I respect professionally and like personally, is not alone in using the Internet to put space between him and his readers. A lot of the Internet marketing gurus, maybe even most of the gurus, do it.

I can't blame them, and I understand their reasons: these are busy guys, they make a lot of money, and their time is limited.

But I take the opposite approach: I make myself directly available to my readers as much as is humanly possible.

My old friend, marketing guru Jeffrey Lant, referred to this as being the "accessible expert."

If you've ever tried to contact me, you know I promptly answer all e-mails I receive...and if you call me, it rings the phone on my desk which I pick up and personally answer.

Being so available to my readers is a deliberate choice on my part. I am not saying I am right to be so reachable, or that X and his ilk are wrong to put so much distance between themselves and their customers.

All I can tell you is that being an "accessible expert" works better for me for several reasons.

>> First, although I'm pretty busy, perhaps I am not as busy and in demand as Mr. X. So while keeping the lines of communication open with my subscribers can sometimes be challenging, it is certainly manageable. So I do it.

>> Second, my readers like being able to communicate with me directly and easily. I know, because they tell me so. And my philosophy is to do, within reason, what my customers want.

>> Third, it's the way I want to be treated by the marketers I buy from. I am frustrated by customer-unfriendly voice mail systems that make it a trial to reach the person I want. And it irritates me when a marketer shields himself from e-mail communication.

So how accessible do you have to be to please your customers while still having a private life? Here's what I recommend:

1–Publish your phone number prominently on your Website and in your e-mail signature file. Make it easy for people to call you.

2–When your phone rings, answer it, and give the time of day to people who call.

Full disclosure: I do have caller ID. So when I am on a copywriting deadline for a client, I do not pick up—and instead let your call go to voice mail. But once I'm free again, I return the call—on my dime.

3—If an e-mail from a customer asks a question which I can reasonably answer in a minute or two, I answer it—for free. No charge.

4—If an e-mail from a customer asks a question that is answered in one of my publications, I send my correspondent a link to it. If it's free, I invite him to download it at no cost. If it costs money, I suggest he buy it.

5—If a customer asks a question that is complex or requires a customized answer tailored to his specific situation, I tell him that to solve the problem for him falls under consulting and explain the cost.

Regarding point #4, a few of my customers have complained that I am a money-grubber for telling them to buy an information product when they ask me a question.

I do not agree with their criticism. If the answer to your question is clearly articulated and well thought out on page 187 of my book, I assert that it is reasonable and sensible for me to suggest you buy the book, turn to page 187, and read the answer there. Why should I have to spend my time writing a long e-mail to you without compensation, when I have already taken time to prepare the answer for you in advance—and when my book buyers have had to pay for the same content?

Regarding point #5, one thing that really irks me is that subscribers who ask me questions that clearly require customized analysis by me virtually never offer to pay me for my time and knowledge. They never bring up money, because they hope and pray I will be a dupe and just answer without charge.

Unfortunately for me, I have to pay my son's tuition at Carnegie-Mellon, and I have only 24 hours in a day, both of which make me disinclined to work for free. When the guy who comes to my house to fix my busted washing machine does it for free, then I will reconsider my position.

My biggest pet peeve is subscribers who send me a link to their Website, and ask me to look at it and tell them my opinion...without any offer to pay me for the critique. Again, when my doctor starts giving me exams for free, I will reconsider my position.

8

There is No Shortcut on the Road to Success

Subscriber MN writes, "I'm thinking of doing an online business. Approximately what would you charge to create the product, copywriting, landing page, everything A-Z? Or can you recommend an existing package where everything is already done that I can buy?"

I have some bad news for MN. What he wants—a complete "done for you," online business-in-a-box—and by that I mean one that: (a) he can actually afford and (b) would actually work—does not exist.

Everyone wants the quick and easy way out. No one wants to do the hard work. They want to wave a magic wand or rub a lucky rabbit's foot—and be handed the online business they seek on a platter, already revved up and spitting out profits. Sorry, but it ain't happening, MN.

Reminds me of the scene in "A League of Their Own" where Geena Davis wants to play baseball but complains to Tom Hanks that the baseball life is too hard.

Tom snaps back: "It's supposed to be hard. If it wasn't hard, everyone would do it. The hard...is what makes it great."

I think that's the case with entrepreneurship in general and starting an Internet marketing business in particular.

The promoters promise it's easy because—hey—we copywriters know that "easy" sells.

But building a successful online business isn't easy. In theory it is simple. In practice—often tricky as heck.

Oh, in some ways DOING the business is physically easy—you can work at home and make a good living devoting only an hour or two a day to it.

I don't have employees. I don't have big overhead. I don't talk with customers on the phone or face to face. So in that respect having an Internet business is not too stressful.

But it is not always easy to figure it all out, put the pieces together, and make them make money.

Those of us in the business are constantly learning and studying, and continually fine-tuning our e-mails, landing pages, products, offers, ads, and just about everything else.

There isn't a day goes by that I am not reading blogs, trade magazines, and online newsletters in a frantic effort to keep up to speed on what's new in Internet marketing.

Most of what I learn I will never use. But since I don't know what will be the next breakthrough until I learn and try it—I am learning all the time.

To answer MN's question: no, he cannot hire me or anyone else to create the whole business for him, get it running, and then hand it over to him to enjoy.

That's because if I or anyone else puts in all that effort, we'd make MUCH more money by just keeping that business and running it ourselves than we could selling it to someone else, no matter how much they offered us for it.

Yes, there are some promoters advertising "done for you" Internet businesses-in-a-box. I haven't reviewed them all and so cannot comment on them all.

But the ones I have seen are thin. Typically the quality of the products and promotions they sell you is pretty pitiful—a lot sell 5-page e-books some Elance freelancer probably wrote for ten bucks—and the business is not actually making money for anyone but the promoter selling it to others.

Again, if the products and landing pages the promoter was selling really pulled in the dollars online, he'd be buying as much traffic as he could to drive buyers to the micro sites...and making his money on product sales...not trying to pawn the whole kit and caboodle off to unsuspecting prey like MN.

9

Confessions of a Former Book Publishing Snob

I'm afraid that when I tell you what I am about to tell you, you'll either be offended or think I'm a jerk.

But, because I always tell you the complete and unvarnished truth about the subjects we discuss, I'm going to go ahead and tell you anyway.

So here it goes: for more years than I can count, I secretly looked down upon people who self-published their books.

I was a mainstream book publishing elitist and snob.

Before you start throwing rotten tomatoes at me or call me a Philistine, remember that I grew up in the traditional book publishing world...and so that was what I knew and loved.

If I had self-published my first book, I might well have become a self-publishing cheerleader.

But as it happened, when I wrote my first book proposal in 1981, the first agent I took it to agreed to represent it...and the first publisher he showed it to, McGraw-Hill, bought it for an $8,500 advance (and it was a short book).

For all my books since then...more than 80 to date...I have had them published by mainstream publishing houses including John Wiley & Sons,

HarperCollins, Henry Holt, Prentice Hall, and New American Library.

I always preferred traditional publishing to self-publishing for these reasons:

1–It was a lot less work. I only had to write the book. The publisher took care of designing, printing, storing, shipping, and selling it.

2–It cost me nothing out of pocket. And it paid me immediate income–an advance–even before the book was published.

3–There was much more prestige in those days being published by a "real" publishing house than by having it printed at your own expense.

At least one famous self-publishing guru disputes me on this. He says: "The reader doesn't look to see or care about who published the book; he only cares who the author is and what the book is about."

From years of personal experience, I can tell you flat-out that this isn't true–and people are more impressed when you are published by a traditional publisher...regardless of whether they should be.

Once, when I was giving a speaking engagement, one of the attendees volunteered to chauffer me from the airport to the convention center–because, he told me, doing so would give him some private time with me.

"So you've written 35 books?" he asked me.

"Yep," I replied.

"Self-published them, I suppose," he said lightly, but I could hear the undertone of something like mockery or mild denigration in his voice.

"Nope," I snapped backed proudly and confidently. "My publishers are McGraw-Hill, Prentice Hall, and Wiley."

He looked at me with newfound respect, and the only reason was that in his eyes I was now a "real" author instead of a guy that paid to have his scribbling printed and bound.

But today, book publishing is a lot different than what it was in 1981. Here's how I see your book publishing options in 2013:

1–Sell your book to a mainstream publisher.

The traditional book publishing industry has been beaten down in a dozen different ways–from the Kindle to the growing preference for online video over print.

However, I maintain that if you are writing books to build your reputation and gain prestige in your field, the best option is still to go with a traditional publisher...even though the advances get smaller with each passing year.

2–Self-publish a paper book.

This is still less prestigious than having your book come out under a major publisher's imprint, but it's a viable option if you either can't or don't want to sell your book to a John Wiley or McGraw-Hill.

You keep a greater percentage of the revenues from the sale of each copy, and you buy your own inventory at a much lower cost per copy than the 50% author's discount major publishers give their authors.

3–Kindle e-book.

There are a number of advantages to doing a Kindle e-book not available with other formats.

First, it's dirt-cheap. Just create an electronic file in the format required by Kindle and you are good to go. It's a no-brainer.

Second, by investing a few hundred bucks or so in professional cover and page design, when your Kindle e-book is posted on Amazon, it looks as good and professional as any traditionally published book being sold on the site.

Third, there's no real commitment of time or money. You can publish and promote a Kindle e-book as aggressively as any other book. Or just pop it up there and see what happens.

The book you are reading is my second self-published Kindle e-book, and I think I will do more in the future.

Today when you publish a Kindle e-book, Amazon has an easy-to-use service called CreateSpace that lets you print some nice-looking paperbacks for not too much money–as many or as few as you want. It also gives online buyers the option of ordering a paperback, which is shipped by Amazon, instead of the Kindle version.

10

A Shortcut to Learning New Skills

This is so embarrassing I hesitated to tell you about it.

But since I think it contains a helpful idea, I am telling you now.

A few weeks ago, we moved, and there is a bowling alley not too far down the road.

My family got excited about bowling and of course I love to do things with them.

Problem is, I had not been in a bowling alley for over 40 years.

So I worried that I had forgotten how to bowl and would absolutely suck at it.

I was right.

The first game I bowled a pathetic 92, and would have scored even lower, except I got two consecutive strikes near the end.

There were several gutter balls involved in this disaster.

Now, I hate doing things I am not good at.

And since I am not good at most things, that severely limits my activities.

But I wanted to bowl with my family and at least be good enough so I was not humiliated when I did.

My solution: After my pathetic 92 game, I walked up to the front counter and asked whether they offered bowling lessons.

Turns out they have a former pro bowler who does. I immediately signed up and, amazing to me at age 56, am taking bowling lessons.

My goal is not to be a great bowler. I just want to learn the basics so I feel confident when I step up and roll the ball.

Why am I telling you this?

Because throughout our lives come times when we need or want to be able to do something and find we don't know how.

Many people struggle through it. But I don't: I immediately seek out help, whether it's a coach, consultant, teacher, mentor, or a trainer. I quickly find someone who can teach me what I need to know, and immediately hire them to do so.

Lots of people hem and haw, promise to learn the skill, and never get around to it.

Hiring a consultant, coach, or trainer gets you going fast, because they don't pussyfoot around. If you have weekly lessons, like I do in bowling, you progress faster than simply doing it whenever you can or feel like it.

Second, the expert shows you the mistakes to avoid and the right steps to take, getting you to your goal that much faster.

There is often hesitation in hiring a consultant, coach, or teacher because of the cost. But virtually every time I have done so, it has been worth many times the fee I paid.

My father bowled in a league. With a 167 average, he was one of the lower-ranked bowlers in the league. For me, a 167 would be beyond my wildest dreams. My bowling coach's son is 19 and an absolute whiz: he has bowled two 300 games and three 299 games, and was asked to join the pro tour. But he is going to college first.

11

Do Authors Owe You the Time of Day?

My readers often complain to me that the gurus they follow are aloof and inaccessible.

You often can't reach them by phone...and either you get no reply to your e-mail or an automated reply from an auto-responder.

My readers say this is rude—and it angers them.

After all, they bought the guru's book or course...or might someday soon.

Doesn't this entitle the customer to some personal time and customized advice from the guru himself?

Well—yes and no.

I personally answer my own phone...and reply to my own e-mail messages.

But I don't think other authors and info marketers are obligated to do so (though I think they should).

When you buy a Stephen King novel, you understand that he is not obligated to discuss the plot with you—and most likely will not do so.

In the same way, when you buy a business book for $20, you are purchasing the contents—and nothing beyond that.

The author may also consult and speak, but he charges thousands of dollars for those services...and just buying his book doesn't entitle you to them, right?

One famous copywriting guru complained to me that some of his readers have the unmitigated gall to call him up, ask for free advice, and then grumble when they don't get it.

"Do they not realize my paying clients get first dibs on my time?" he asked me.

I do. It makes sense to me. And I hope to you too. But still, I desire to help my readers as much as I can while still having time for a life.

So how do I respond to queries and complaints, both phone and e-mail, without becoming overwhelmed—and unable to get my work done?

For e-mail queries and complaints, about 90% are routine (e.g., did not receive a product they ordered on my Website, can't open the PDF of an e-book, need help becoming an affiliate, etc.).

These I pass on to my assistant, because she can handle them better than I can.

About 10% require a more thoughtful answer. These I answer myself—either via e-mail or sometimes a brief phone call.

Tip: when a customer has a problem or complaint they register via e-mail, calling them on the phone and helping them one-on-one converts them from complainers into rabid fans.

They are shocked that you actually took the time to call—and care enough to resolve their problem personally.

Of course, I can't talk to everyone all the time: I have copy to write for my clients.

So I use caller ID to screen my inbound phone calls.

After the call, I listen to the voice mail.

If it's routine, I pass the request or complaint on to my assistant for handling.

If it's a situation where my personal attention would add value or create satisfaction, I will call back and help them.

However, as an information marketer, you want to avoid the trap of allowing people you don't know to pump you endlessly for free consulting over the phone.

Speaker Patricia Fripp has a great technique for handling these brain-pickers which I use.

When someone who is not a client wants to ask me questions, I say: "My time normally sells for $500 an hour. I will give you 5 minutes–starting now."

This script makes the caller understand that your time is limited...and that by talking with them without charge, you are doing them a favor and giving them something of value.

Five minutes may not seem like much. But at $500 an hour, 5 minutes of my time is worth almost $42. That's a generous gift to give a total stranger.

The time limit also forces callers to get to the point, not waste your time with long explanations, and listen to what you tell them without debate or argument.

Here's another way you, as an expert, can save time answering questions from readers...

Produce content—an FAQ page on your Website, a blog, a newsletter, a special report, an information product—on the topics you are asked about most often.

Then, when people ask you for advice on Topic X, give them the URL of the Website where they can either read your content for free...or purchase your information product on Topic X.

Am I clear on how to handle inquiries from clients, customers, prospects, readers, and fans?

If not, I expect you'll call or e-mail me for clarification—and I welcome hearing from you.

12

Why You Should Never Give Unsolicited Advice

The other day I got an e-mail from JT, a professional proofreader, who expressed her grave concern that she had found more than one typo among the dozens of Websites I own.

"Can I be direct without being offensive?" asks JT. "Let me start by saying that my only reason for writing these e-mails is that I want to work with you, because I think we could both benefit from collaboration."

JT continues: "You need a new proofreader–and if you do your own proofreading, you need to fire yourself from that job!"

Did I hire JT as my new proofreader?

No, because I did, in fact, find her e-mail to be both offensive and self-serving.

Yet many freelancers and independent contractors who render creative, professional, and technical services take a similar approach to marketing. And it almost never works.

The basis of this horribly inappropriate and ineffective selling method is: approach complete strangers...point out a fault with something they are doing...and then offer your services to help them fix the defect.

On the surface, it seems sensible. After all, you are doing someone a favor by helping them correct a defect that could be hurting their business, right?

So you'd naturally think they'd be grateful, and reciprocate by hiring you to fix the problem you alerted them to.

After all, you have already demonstrated your expertise, skill, and value by detecting the problem for them without charge.

But here's the problem: most folks, including me, don't like unsolicited advice.

One of the inviolate rules of my life, both business and personal, is: never give unsolicited advice.

Advice is only valued if three conditions exist: (1) the advice is sought after (i.e., they asked for it), (2) it is positive and not negative or insulting to the recipient, and (3) it is constructive and specific.

JT's e-mail to me violated the first and second of these conditions.

First, I didn't ask her to proofread for me. So why do it?

The fact that she is spending her time proofreading copy for strangers without compensation tells me she probably isn't very busy—and that she needs more business.

Your prospects prefer to work with vendors who are successful and in demand...not with those they perceive as desperate and needy.

Second, she insults me—telling me I am a lousy proofreader and I should "fire" myself.

Customers buy from people they like. And we don't like people who insult us.

Another problem with trying to win business by giving unsolicited critiques or advice to strangers is that you risk looking ignorant.

That's because you lack the background on their situation to know whether your suggestions are valid and warranted.

In JT's case, she assumed we had a typo on a landing page because we are bad proofreaders.

She's wrong. The real reason why you can find typos on some of my sites is that I have literally hundreds of pages posted on the Web.

And with my team already overloaded, we simply can't always keep up with our proofreading and other tasks that are not critical to sales.

A better approach for JT would have been to point out the typo, and then say, "Are your proofreaders overloaded? Hire me to take on the backlog and get those pesky typos off your sites forever."

That would have been more appealing to me than assuming we stink at proofreading, which we don't.

Finally, JT's idea of giving unsolicited advice to strangers violates the Silver Rule of Marketing, first articulated to me by marketing consultant Pete Silver.

Peter told me: "It is always better to get them to come to you, rather than for you to go to them."

By violating this rule and soliciting my business, JT placed herself in a weak position.

It may be that I don't care about typos (not true, but there are people who don't), in which case JT is pursuing an unqualified prospect.

Even if I *had* been interested in her offer, JT would have to work hard to convince me that she is the proofreader I should hire.

After all, I've never heard of her before, have no idea who she is, and therefore certainly do not perceive her as an expert or top pro in editing and proofreading.

On the other hand, if you get prospects to come to you because of your reputation as a recognized expert or top pro in your field, you don't have to do a lot of convincing or selling, because these prospects are already predisposed to hire you.

I would advise JT to stop wasting her time criticizing the Websites of marketers who don't want those critiques and may even resent them.

Instead, she should take steps—write a column on proper English for a respected business magazine, create a course on copyediting, speak at conferences on the importance of proper business English—that position her as an expert in correct writing.

By doing so, I might have come running to JT for help, instead of running away from her.

13

The One and Only Thing You Need to Succeed

The other day, my oldest son expressed to me his concern that he would not be successful as an adult.

Why not? Because (in his mind), there are quite a number of things he isn't good at (math is at the top of the list).

I shared with him an encouraging success secret that I now pass on to you.

Namely, that to be extremely successful—in business, career, and wealth building—you don't have to be good at a lot of things.

In fact, you can attain an extremely high level of success even if you are really good at only one thing.

Warren Buffett made this point some years ago in a college lecture he gave with Bill Gates.

He said, in essence, that he (Buffett) is not very strong, not very fast, not very physical, not very athletic.

"If I was dropped in the middle of Africa, I'd be eaten by a lion within 2 minutes," he told the audience.

However, because he is good at only one thing—investing in the stock market—Buffett is an extremely wealthy man.

In my neighborhood, parents worry incessantly about whether their kids will be successful.

They fret over the kids' grades ... piano lessons ... sports ... extra-curricular activities ... even how many friends the kids have ... summer camp ... you name it.

My kids have it easy, because I don't worry about any of these things.

As long as they do their best, I don't obsess over their grades or what extra-curricular activities they should be doing but are not.

I tell them what I just told you...

Find the one thing in life that you love—that turns you on, that you are passionate about—and keep doing it.

The more you do it, as Michael Masterson has pointed out, the better you get at it.

With an early start and years of practice, your kids will get good at the one thing they love, become extremely competent, and therefore never have to worry about supporting themselves or being out of a job.

Of course, to ensure financial success, this "one thing"—the singular passion—must be something others will pay money for.

To paraphrase Aristotle, "Where your passions intersect with the needs of the public, therein lies your vocation."

Like Warren Buffett, I have very few talents and am not good at most things.

The list of what I am mediocre or bad at is very long indeed.

I'm incompetent at fixing things around the house, for example.

And I have a depth-perception problem that makes me lousy at tennis, baseball, or any sport where you have to hit a ball with a stick.

But I was always a voracious reader. I love books, reading, and writing. I began to write early–amateur comic books in elementary school, short stories in junior high school, articles for the papers in high school and college.

I spent so much time in college writing for our paper–it was a daily, and I became the features editor–that my writing began to improve significantly.

I realized that was the one thing I love to do, have an aptitude for, and am good at.

And in copywriting, I found an area of writing where I could be paid handsomely for my efforts.

A mistake many people make is to continually work to improve themselves in areas where they are weak.

What you should do instead is to improve yourself in the one area where you are strongest.

Why?

Today we are a society of specialists.

When I was a kid, and the tiles in our bathroom began to crumble, my dad strapped on a tool belt and fixed them.

Today when my bathroom has a cracked tile, I call the tile guy–and pay him to fix it.

Success does not come from being a jack of all trades, and a master of none.

It comes from mastery of a skill or body of knowledge that others—an employer or customer—will pay you to share.

If I were to take a course in tiling, I would learn a little...but my abilities would be nothing compared to my tile guy, who has been doing this for 40 years.

I spend my time increasing my knowledge of marketing, which helps me make more money in my freelance copywriting and Internet marketing business.

Society admires the Renaissance man, the well-rounded individual.

But more often than not, it's the singularly focused individual—Bill Gates, Warren Buffett, Tiger Woods—the person who is exceedingly good at just one thing—who reaps the greatest rewards.

14

What Do You Do?

An "elevator pitch" is a 30-second answer to the question, "What do you do?"

You need an elevator pitch because the question "What do you do?" is usually asked by complete strangers in casual circumstances.

In these situations, you do not have a captive audience watching you go through your PowerPoint sales presentation.

So your answer must be pithy and to the point.

Why does it matter how you answer the question "What do you do?" when speaking to someone you don't know?

Because you never know when the person you're speaking to is a potential customer or referral source.

Most elevator pitches, unfortunately, don't work— because they are straightforward descriptions of job functions and titles, generating not much else aside from disinterest and a few yawns.

For example, a fellow I met at a party told me, "I am a certified financial planner with more than 20 years experience working."

Yawn.

My friend sales trainer Paul Karasik has an antidote to the deadly dull elevator pitch.

Karasik's three-part formula can enable you to quickly construct the perfect elevator pitch.

By "perfect," I mean an elevator pitch that concisely communicates the value your product or service offers–in a manner that engages rather than bores the other person.

What is the formula?

The first part is to ask a question beginning with the words "Do you know?"

The question identifies the pain or need that your product or service addresses.

For a financial planner who, say, works mostly with middle-aged women who are separated, divorced, widowed, and possibly re-entering the workplace, this question might be:

"Do you know how when women get divorced or re-enter the workforce after many years of depending on a spouse, they are overwhelmed by all the financial decisions they have to make"?

The second part of the formula is a statement that begins with the words "What I do" or "What we do"– followed by a clear description of the service you deliver.

Continuing with our financial planner, she might say: "What we do is help women gain control of their finances and achieve their personal financial and investment goals."

The third part of the formula presents a big benefit and begins "so that."

Here's what the whole thing sounds like:

"Do you know how when women get divorced or re-enter the workforce after many years of depending on a spouse, they are overwhelmed by all the financial decisions they have to make?

"What we do is help women gain control of their finances and achieve their personal financial and investment goals, so that they can stay in the house they have lived in all their lives, have enough income to enjoy a comfortable lifestyle, and be free of money worries."

Action step: construct your elevator pitch today or tonight using Paul Karasik's three-part formula.

>> First part: ask a question beginning with the words "Do you know?" that identifies the pain or need that your product or service addresses.

>> Second part: describe your service, beginning with the words "What I do" or "What we do."

>> Third part: explain why your service is valuable by describing the benefits it delivers, beginning with the words "So that."

15

Are You Too Old to Start a New Career?

At what age are you too old to start an Internet marketing business—or other new career or business?

I have thought at various times in my life (I am now 54) that the cut-off age was 50...60 ...or even 70.

There were two reasons I believed you'd reach a point where starting over just wasn't practical anymore.

The first, and lesser, was sheer age and lifespan: the idea that when there are many more years behind you than ahead of you, your time to enjoy the fruits of whatever labors you pursue is too limited.

The second reason I believed there was a cut-off date for starting a new career, learning a new trade, or launching a new small business was lack of experience.

For instance, one of the many careers I considered in my youth was the law. But years ago, I decided pursuing that was impractical (not that I was really interested anyway; it was more of a theoretical consideration).

Reason: say hypothetically you were to graduate law school at age 45.

You compete against two groups.

The first is other 45-year-old lawyers who are the same age as you—but have 20 years of law experience vs. your zero years.

The other group you compete against is your classmates. Like you, they are new to the law.

But being in their 20s and single, instead of 45 and having a mortgage and 3 kids in college, they can afford to work for starting salaries too small to meet your needs.

However, actor Abe Vigoda has changed my mind about all this...and my opinion today is that it is never too late to learn new things, start a new business, switch careers, or go into a different industry.

Abe Vigoda, if the name does not ring a bell, is the dour-faced actor famous for playing the character Fish on the TV show "Barney Miller."

A few years ago, I read a short interview with Vigoda, who was, at the time, still a working actor at age 87.

In it, I was reminded that Abe Vigoda's big break was his first movie, "The Godfather," in which he played Sal Tessio.

Well, "The Godfather" was released in 1972. So if you do the math, Abe Vigoda didn't begin his movie acting career until he was over 50.

More impressive is that, at age 87, Abe Vigoda–who, pardon me, has a slightly cadaverous appearance that makes him look ready for the Old Folks Home–was still a competitive handball player.

If Abe Vigoda can get his first movie role at over 50–beating out actors his age who had decades more credentials and experience–then I am convinced that you and I can start a new career or business at any age.

Yes, you may have some disadvantages over your younger colleagues, peers, and competitors–including (possibly) less energy, less flexibility, and less adaptability to new technologies and methods.

Then again, maybe not. It depends on your personality–and your circumstances. If you are a retired empty-nester, you may actually have more time, freedom, and flexibility, not less.

On the other hand, if you are still working for a paycheck because you have to and not because you want to, it may take a greater degree of courage and fortitude to make any major business, career, or life change.

As an older entrepreneur or career changer, you will likely have some advantages over your competitors– such as greater life experience and wisdom to draw upon when making decisions.

But I know from first-hand experience that 50 is not too old to make a major change, and from that, I am guessing that your age won't stop you, either.

For example, I started a small online information marketing business as I was closing in on my 50th birthday.

Today I earn a six-figure passive income selling information products on the Internet, "working" less than an hour a day.

In my case, I kept my day job as a freelance copywriter and still put in long hours on that.

But entering a new field–Internet marketing–has energized and renewed me in a way I never thought possible.

If your gut tells you that you are ready for a change, you probably are.

I close with this piece of wisdom from Milton Hershey, founder of Hershey Chocolate:

"I have often been asked–What is the best age for producing? I know only one answer, the age you are now."

16

The Trouble With Personal Preferences

Recently JN, one of my readers, sent me an e-mail very similar in sentiment to dozens of other e-mails I have received over the years.

"Why do marketers like ETR and AWAI send me 16-page DM packages when the copywriter could have said the same thing in 1 to 2 pages?" JN writes.

"The prospect might even buy out of gratitude for not having to wade through those 16 pages and breathe a sigh of relief instead of snarl a nasty expletive."

But JN is not through lambasting long-copy direct marketing yet. Her e-mail continues:

"My brother-in-law makes a hobby of going through those 16-page packages just for fun, red-penciling errors before he tosses them. He would never, under pain of death, buy from a DM package."

And it's not just JN's brother-in-law who thinks direct marketing copywriters are fools.

"My sister just drops those 16-page mailings in the recycling without even bothering to open them," JN reports.

"Many of the people I know feel the same way. So why do copywriters persist in creating these massive multi-page mailings? Because they are paid by the page?

Or because the client wants his pound of flesh from his writers?"

Finally, JN turns to the Internet as the harbinger of doom for long copy, asking, "Isn't the Internet killing off traditional direct response copywriting?"

The answer to JN's question is fairly simple...

The marketers she complains about use long copy not because they love writing it...or paying their copywriters a fortune to write it for them...or because they enjoy spending more money on printing and postage.

They use long copy for only one reason: it works.

Now, does long copy always out-pull short copy?

Of course not.

But long copy often out-pulls short copy when:

>> You are marketing information products or other products that are sold by telling stories or conveying ideas.

>> You are generating a direct sale...via mail order...rather than just generating a lead or inquiry.

>> The reader is unfamiliar with your product and its benefits.

>> You are demanding payment with order. The prospect has to pay up front with a check or credit card. He cannot order the product on credit and get an invoice he can choose to pay–or not pay–later.

>> The product is complex and therefore requires a lot of explanation.

>> The product is something people want rather than something they need–it is a discretionary purchase.

>> The product is expensive, representing an expenditure the prospect is likely to consider carefully before ordering.

As for JN's theory that the Internet is making traditional long-copy direct marketing obsolete, it's quite the opposite: a product that requires long copy to sell offline usually requires long copy to sell online as well.

For instance, take a look at my Website www.myveryfirstebook.com.

So...what does this long copy vs. short copy debate have to do with "the worst way to make marketing decisions"?

Simply that it illustrates that the worst way to make marketing decisions—which is what JN and her family are doing—is through subjective judgment.

Copywriter Peter Beutchel advises marketers: "Don't let personal preferences get in the way."

What's important is not what you think, like, believe, or prefer...it's what your prospects think, like, believe, and prefer.

The poor general advertisers! They are largely stuck having to make subjective judgments about marketing campaigns.

Reason: most general advertisers cannot precisely measure the ROMD (return on marketing dollars) for their ads and commercials.

But direct marketers don't have to rely solely on subjective judgment. We don't have to let our personal likes and dislikes cloud our judgment, like JN's brother-in-law.

That's because direct marketers can put almost any proposition—e.g., headline "A" vs. headline "B," or long copy vs. short copy—to a direct test with an A/B split.

So, JN, it doesn't matter what your sister or brother-in-law do...or that they don't like long copy.

What matters is that in a statistically valid split test, the long copy generated more orders than the short copy.

I close with this quote from advertising legend Claude Hopkins: "Advertising arguments should only be settled by testing, not arguments around a conference table."

17

Beware of Armchair Experts

Many entrepreneurs I meet—even mom-and-pops and SOHOs—spend thousands of dollars on hiring so-called experts to advise them on how to make their businesses more successful.

Sometimes, the expert's advice works out, the investment is recouped, and the entrepreneur is better off for consulting with a professional.

Other times, the expert's advice is either useless or wrong. The client has thrown thousands of dollars he can't afford to lose down the drain, and sees no improvement in his bottom line, productivity, efficiency, or operations.

Since I am frequently on both sides of the table—I sell my services as a copywriter and consultant, and also buy lots of services for my little Internet marketing business—I have a small bit of advice that might save you this agony...and enable you to select advisors who can actually help you.

In my experience, there are 3 types of experts for hire.

The first type of expert I call the *teacher*.

"Teachers" are those who give training, speeches, and seminars...write books and blogs and columns...sell their expertise as consultants or coaches—but don't actually practice what they preach.

You know the expression "those who can do; those who can't teach."

I don't think it's always true...but these teachers have never, for the most part, proven that they can do what they talk about.

That's because mainly they've only taught it or advised others how to do it, but have never done it themselves.

An example of a "teacher expert" is Peter Drucker.

He is revered as a management guru, and writes endless books and gives speech after speech advising CEOs on how to be great managers and leaders.

But by his own admission, he has never been the chief executive of any company.

(Running your own consulting business does not count.)

The second type of expert is the *practitioner*.

This is someone who knows a particular skill or area because he does it—and does it successfully—rather than writes books or articles about it.

An example is Gary Bencivenga, who is arguably one of the greatest copywriters who ever lived.

Yet until his retirement, Gary—to the best of my knowledge—never wrote a book, article, or column on marketing. Nor was he a speaker at marketing conferences.

The third type of expert is the *teacher/practitioner*—an active practitioner who is also a writer, speaker, and teacher in his area of expertise.

A good example of this is Michael Masterson, who writes best-selling books on business success and entrepreneurship–based on his decades of experience building and growing many successful companies.

Some of the many companies he has been involved with generate annual sales ranging from $10 million to $100 million–and beyond.

Now, as to which type of experts you should hire–and when...

If you are a seminar organizer or meeting planner, most of your speakers are probably teachers.

That's because speaking is how they make their living, and so they are actively seeking these speaking engagements. And, they are good speakers.

(Many practitioners for the most part shun speaking requests; they are too busy making money running their companies.)

You may think hiring a professional speaker to give a professional speech makes sense.

After all, you want someone who knows the topic and can communicate it in a clear, motivating, and entertaining fashion.

The problem is that the teacher's knowledge is all theoretical: gleaned from research and observation and thinking, but not actually doing.

Therefore, the teacher *thinks* he knows what works...but in reality, he is just making educated guesses.

MA, a professional speaker who also owned and operated several successful insurance agencies, once said that nobody should be a full-time speaker—because if you are not practicing what you preach, you really don't know what you are talking about.

Yes, you can hire a teacher as your seminar presenter or keynote speaker.

Many can deliver a rousing talk that gets a standing ovation and great evaluations.

But their expertise rarely extends beyond the content of the talk. And this shallowness inevitably comes through in both their presentation and their interaction with attendees after they step down from the platform.

If you are a small business owner hiring expert advisors and professionals—copywriters, strategists, consultants, and advisors—you should never hire pure teachers.

Think about it. Let's say you want to hire someone to manage a pay-per-click ad campaign for your company.

Do you really want to take the advice from someone who has, over his lifetime, done fewer actual PPC ad campaigns than you have?

Someone who has just written a book based on studying the PPC campaigns of others—real entrepreneurs with the guts to actually put their own money where their mouth is?

The bottom line?

Your key business advisors and vendors should all be practitioners or practitioner/teachers.

First and foremost, they should have long experience—and a terrific track record—in the discipline for which you seek their help.

For this purpose, either a practitioner or a practitioner/teacher will do nicely.

The one advantage of the practitioner/teacher over the practitioner is an enhanced ability to clearly and efficiently explain what he is doing...so his clients can learn and—over time—become more self sufficient.

I once heard the definition of an expert as someone who doesn't necessarily know more than other people, but their information is better organized.

A practitioner expert, however, does know more than other people—because he has learned from real-world trial and error.

A teaching expert, on the other hand, usually does not know more—because his knowledge is gleaned from studying practitioners who do know more.

But the teacher's information is better organized as a result of putting it into a seminar, workshop, or book.

As for the practitioner/teachers, they can in some instances give you the best of both worlds.

As their client, you get the expert's in-depth experience and authoritative knowledge of the subject in which they advise you.

You also benefit from the expert's ability to help you both understand what they are doing (and why) as well as educate you in their field.

That way, you can learn over time to do more and more on your own—if you are so inclined.

18

Avoid This Flub That Makes You Look Foolish

Many years ago, I taught a class at the Learning Annex in New York City on how to make a six-figure income as a freelancer.

One student, JR, wanted to break into writing TV commercials for Madison Avenue, and he had devised what was (according to him) a brilliant marketing strategy for getting hired.

In actuality, it was the second-worst marketing idea I'd ever heard in my life.

JR had, he told the class, written some "brilliant" TV commercials.

The Super Bowl was only a few weeks away at the time.

JR's marketing strategy would be to show up at the offices of Madison Avenue's biggest ad agencies and show the copy for his commercials to the creative director.

The creative director, he reasoned, was under tremendous pressure to produce a great Super Bowl commercial for the agency's clients.

By bringing those great commercials with him, JR would save the day—and be hired at an enormous salary to write for the agency.

Of course, this is a terrible idea for all the obvious reasons:

>> With the Super Bowl only a few weeks away, all the commercials had been written and shot weeks or months earlier—and were already in the can.

>> The creative director has never heard of JR. She doesn't know who JR is or whether he has any qualifications or talent. So the chances of the creative director agreeing to see JR are miniscule to none.

>> JR has no knowledge of which of the agency's clients actually are running Super Bowl spots. Even if he did know, he hasn't been briefed on the product positioning or the campaign strategy...so how can he possibly write a commercial that achieves the client's marketing objective?

I gently told JR—and the rest of the class—that doing work on spec for a client who hasn't asked you to do so is an absolute waste of time.

However, stupid as it is, there is a marketing strategy that's even worse: giving an unsolicited *critique* of something a potential client has done—a new product design, an ad campaign, a Website—in the hopes of being hired to fix it.

Why is giving a critique even worse than doing work on spec without prior agreement by the potential client to review it?

Well, think about it.

You send a letter to a business telling them their Website stinks...or their customer service people are idiots...or their product is lousy.

There's a good chance that the recipient of your letter is the person responsible for approving that Website, training the customer service staff, or designing the product.

So right away, you have begun the relationship by insulting them—saying, in effect, "You don't know what you are doing."

They probably don't agree with you that they've done a bad job...or else they wouldn't have produced the site, training, or product in the first place.

You come along and give a contrary opinion—highly critical and negative.

They think, "Who the heck are YOU, bub? Why should I listen to what YOU say?"

As they see it, your opinion is subjective, not objective.

It's also self-serving: you are a vendor, so your objective in reaching out to them is to get them to hire you and spend money on your products or services.

Worse, here you are, spending your time reviewing Websites, calling companies who aren't your client, and telling them how bad their sites are—without being paid to do so.

This causes them to think that if you were really any good at what you do, you'd be swamped with projects—and not cold calling strangers trying to rustle up work.

I've frequently been on the receiving end of this "you're doing it all wrong and we can help you fix it" marketing strategy—especially from Web designers.

And speaking as a prospect, I can tell you it not only doesn't work with me, but it's also annoying and offensive.

Just last week, I got yet another such call from a Web designer.

"I was looking at your site and it really is poorly designed," TN, the Web designer, told me. "I would love to help you improve its performance."

"Do you know my marketing objective for my Website?" I asked TN.

"Uh, no," he admitted.

"Well, TN," I said quite reasonably. "If you don't know what I want the site to do for my business...and you don't know its current performance metrics...how can you possibly know that you can improve it?

I let him stutter and stammer for a few seconds, before politely ending the call.

My friend RA, who once ran a mail order business selling information products for gamblers, was also a victim of the "you're doing it all wrong and we can help you fix it" marketing gambit.

SH, a newbie freelance copywriter, wrote RA an unsolicited 2-page critique of his latest DM package.

SH closed his letter by suggesting to RA that his marketing results would be greatly improved by letting a "professional copywriter" (like SH) work his magic on it.

RA and I both had a good laugh over this...because RA is universally acknowledged (except by SH, who didn't recognize his name) as one of the top direct response copywriters working today.

Irritated, RA sent SH a testy letter pointing out this fact...and also noting that the package SH thought was so terrible was in fact a blockbuster control–making SH look stupid and silly.

Conclusion: doing a critique OR work on spec for a potential client who has not asked for it seems, on the surface, a sensible approach to marketing your services.

But it is not. In fact, it's the least effective marketing strategy for selling professional services ever devised.

My advice for you when marketing your professional or technical services is as follows:

>> Never give unsolicited advice or criticism.

>> Don't offer solutions until you really know what the problem is–and the only way you can really understand the problem is for the potential client to tell you.

>> If you want to show the potential client how smart you are, stop pontificating. Instead, ask intelligent questions and listen to the answers.

19

School Is Never Out for the Pro

Some time ago, I casually mentioned in my e-newsletter that I was taking a writing course.

One of my readers, JN, was absolutely shocked.

"YOU are taking a WRITING course?" she asked incredulously.

The implication was that–given that I have been a writer for over three decades–my taking a writing course is either frivolous or silly...a waste of time and money.

JN could not be more wrong.

"School is never out for the professional," I answered concisely.

It's my observation that folks who are really at the top of their field are constantly reading, studying, learning, and attending lectures in their specialty.

Why? To raise their mastery and skill to an even higher level.

On the other hand, those who are at the bottom seem to feel they learned everything they need to know at college, trade school, or on the job.

And they exhibit little or no desire to spend more time learning it better.

To me, this attitude seems lazy and counter-productive at best–and dangerous at worst.

Can you imagine going to a doctor who didn't keep up with the latest medical research?

Of course not.

So why is the idea of a writer taking a writing class so surprising?

JN's reaction reminds me of an American Society of Journalists and Authors (ASJA) weekend writing conference I attended many years ago.

The person sitting next to me and I were both studying the curriculum in our conference brochures.

"This looks good," I said, pointing to a page, "a session on how to write book proposals."

She sniffed haughtily.

"I wouldn't need to go to THAT," she said in a snobby, superior tone. "I am ALREADY an author...and I have written a published book."

At the time, I had written 30 published books. But I didn't tell her that.

Instead, I just went to the session. And I learned a lot—enough to sell 50 more books since then (and counting).

Maybe JN thought that, seeing as I presumably know how to write, I would be better off taking a course in flower arranging or bookkeeping or PowerPoint.

But as busy adults, you and I have extremely limited time. We can take only so many courses.

And you will get a far better return on your investment in education by taking courses in things you are already good at—your strengths—rather than areas in which you are weak.

Why?

Your strengths are what make you successful.

The other stuff doesn't much matter.

In his book "Strength Finders" (Gallup Press), Tim Rath writes:

"People have several times more potential for growth when they invest energy in developing their strengths instead of correcting their deficiencies."

Yet, notes Rath, 77% of parents think that a student's lowest grades deserve more time and attention than the subjects the student is best at.

Think about it this way...

In a horse race, the winning horse can earn tens of thousands of dollars more than the horse that "places" or "shows" (comes in #2 or #3).

Yet often, especially in major races, the first-place horse beats the second-place horse by only a fraction of a second.

Therefore, if the horse and jockey make a massive effort to improve in speed, and beat their previous time by only a second or two, they can win instead of place or show—and make the owner and jockey a lot richer.

On the other hand, a racing horse is a lot less powerful, and can pull a lot less weight, than a Clydesdale—those humongous horses that pull the Budweiser beer wagon.

If you strength-trained the racehorse for years, it could probably get stronger.

But it would never get even close to the Clydesdale in strength...and it wouldn't earn a dime more on the track.

Many things about success are counterintuitive, and the notion of training is one of the most counterintuitive of all.

Most people, when they see classes being offered, gravitate toward classes on subjects they are weak in...hoping to improve their skill level from minimal to acceptable, or learning something new.

For instance, I am not an expert in search engine marketing, which is a hot topic in Internet marketing.

So to correct the defect, I signed up for the Direct Marketing Association's Certificate Program in Search Engine Marketing (SEM).

I took the class and learned a lot about search engine marketing–useful for me as a copywriter.

But I have also learned something else...

Namely, that no matter how much I study search engine marketing, I will never know more than a small fraction of what the top gurus–like the ones who wrote the DMA program–know about search engines.

So does that mean I gave up learning SEM ...and did not optimize my Website?

No. I am still learning SEM. And my Website was optimized. But not by me.

Instead, I did something a lot smarter than trying to do it myself.

I went out and found a top SEO consultant, who (with my assistant's help) optimized the site for me. (Although I DID write the copy.)

As you can tell, I am a big believer in specialization and the hiring of specialists.

There is so much to know, no one can know it all. And trying to do so is futile.

As Thomas Edison once said, we don't know one-millionth of one percent about anything.

Given the overwhelming amount of information in the world today, and our increasingly limited time to master it, I am convinced that we get the best ROI on learning and training by focusing on our strengths—and learning to do what we do well even better.

I have found that, with rare exception, most people are only really good at one thing.

In particular, I am wary of professionals with hyphenated expertise (e.g., "writer-designer," "illustrator-photographer"); I find that these folks are usually good at only one of the two designations—and usually mediocre at the other.

I also agree with the late direct mail consultant Dick Benson, who said: "Do what you do best in-house; buy everything else outside."

P.S. The 12-week writing course cost around $500. For each weekly assignment, I wrote an essay. I then turned around and sold these essays, with additional ones

I wrote after the course, to a major publishing house for a $20,000 advance. The essay collection was published by Thomas Nelson under the title "Count Your Blessings."

20

How to Give Gifts

Most businesspeople sweat over giving business gifts to their clients, prospects, and customers.

They don't know what to give.

They do think they know when to give it—but as I will reveal in a minute, they really don't.

They worry about whether the gift is the right gift, how much to spend, and what the recipient will think.

I've escaped this particular trap, mainly because I like to give people little gifts.

I do it for relatives...friends...neighbors...as well as prospects and clients.

My gift-giving method, which has been very successful for me, is simple:

When I stumble across something really cool or neat I think a particular person would enjoy, and it doesn't cost a fortune, I buy it, wrap it, and send it with a note.

I know what each of my clients (and friends, and relatives) likes, because I have a good memory for that sort of thing.

But you don't need a near-photographic memory to remember what people like: just make a note in your database or address book in their record or listing.

The best business gifts relate to the other person's major interests, hobbies, and activities.

I find these things out mainly by talking to them: we usually start business conferences with an exchange of pleasantries, and I ask questions so that I learn what they like.

(I do this not for gift-giving purposes, but because I am genuinely interested. It also helps us find common ground which is a great way to build relationships.)

If you are not comfortable having these conversations with clients, there is another way to find out their likes and dislikes: social networking sites.

Just check their Facebook, Twitter, or MySpace profile to instantly learn their favorite activities and hobbies.

For instance, reading one client's Facebook profile just out of curiosity, we found out she loves to play poker.

When we saw a nice poker set, we couldn't resist: we bought it and sent it as a "thank you" for her being so easy to work with.

The traditional approach to giving business gifts is to send a gift during the holiday season.

The problem with doing so is twofold. First, your gift gets lost in the pile of other gifts that prospect receives from all her other vendors.

Second, it creates an instant expectation in the prospect that she will receive a gift from you every year.

Therefore, if you skip a year, she will feel cheated. You are "stuck" having to give all those gifts to all those customers year after year.

That's why I give business gifts spontaneously...when I come across the perfect item I know a specific client would love...and not according to any schedule or annual milestone such as a birthday or holiday.

According to a research report published by Bulova Watch, one-third of business gifts are given at times other than Christmas—and that has more impact than just another Xmas present.

Does all this gift-giving pay off in terms of improved customer loyalty and repeat business?

It would seem so: the Bulova study reports that 7 out of 10 recipients buy from companies that give them business gifts.

Do not make the gift too lavish, lest it be perceived as a bribe rather than a gift.

When I worked in the defense industry decades ago, there was a $25 limit to the cost of a gift we contractors could give to our customers in the federal government.

Business gifts do not have to be expensive to be appreciated. In fact, people enjoy small gifts, even little ad specialties, that bring a smile to their face.

One of my favorite gifts to give clients and prospects is an autographed copy of one of my books.

When you sign a contract with a publisher to write a book, you usually get ten free author's copies. Ask for 25 so you'll have extras to give away without it costing you anything out of pocket.

The one occasion where I do deliberately time a gift is to say "thank you" for a favor.

For instance, when I have a new book come out, my joint venture partners are kind enough to promote it to their lists.

When they do, I send them a short note, an autographed copy of the book, and a small Starbucks gift card.

I wish I could say they appreciate the book more than the coffee—but I suspect it is often the opposite!

21

Is Marketing Cheating?

Is marketing cheating?

MW seems to think so.

On my blog, she challenged me for saying that my book is an "Amazon best-seller."

MW didn't accuse me outright of lying.

Nor should she, considering my book..."Persuasive Presentations for Business" (Entrepreneur Press)...reached the #2 spot on the Amazon nonfiction best-seller list.

What MW didn't like is that I used e-mail marketing to promote sales of my book on Amazon.

In fact, you may be familiar with the marketing technique I used, which has become known as "The Instant Amazon Best-Seller Formula."

Used by many Internet marketers, including Mary Ellen Tribby and Michael Masterson to name just two, this method was pioneered–I believe–by Joe Vitale.

The way it works is simple...

You send an e-mail to your subscribers promoting your book...and get lots of your joint venture partners and affiliates to do the same.

(By the way, you can read more about the Instant Amazon Best-Seller Formula at www.myamazonbestseller.com.)

You offer subscribers a bribe—a bunch of free bonus reports contributed by you and your partners—as an incentive to buy your book.

Here's the trick: to get the bonus reports, they must purchase the book from Amazon.com on the date you specify.

If they buy it elsewhere...or on another day ...no bonus gifts for them.

That way, the orders all come in on Amazon on the same day, driving your book way up in the Amazon sales rankings for that day.

MW and many other people I have talked with think that the Instant Amazon Best-Seller Formula is somehow cheating—rigging the system to make our books instant temporary best-sellers.

And it's true, we are manipulating the system.

But what's wrong with that?

It's called MARKETING: using promotions (in this case, e-mail) to promote a product (in this case, our books) to increase sales.

Novels by James Patterson are heavily promoted in radio advertising designed to sell more copies.

Does that mean they are somehow not "real" best-sellers, because they were advertised?

Same thing with Oprah...

If your publicist gets your book into the Oprah Book Club, you are almost guaranteed an instant best-seller.

So why is it perfectly legitimate to advertise your book on radio or in the newspaper...or publicize it on

TV...but a "no-no" to e-mail your subscribers (who have opted into your list because they are actually interested in what you write)?

Answer: Because e-mail marketing is direct marketing.

And direct marketing has always had an image problem with the press and the public.

After all, direct mail is called "junk mail."

So why aren't TV commercials called "junk TV"?

It is true that a small percentage of products sold through direct marketing have been of questionable value, quality, or legitimacy.

But that doesn't make direct marketing uniquely sleazy vs. other forms of sales and marketing.

A small percentage of businesses in every distribution channel and industry are crooked and take advantage of unwary consumers.

For instance, it was mainly Madison Avenue that told us we'd be cool and popular if we smoked cigarettes.

And it is general advertising, not direct marketing, that has our kids growing obese and unfit on fast food French fries and sugar-filled junk food.

Because direct marketing often relies on long copy to make the sale, there are many folks who tell me they find long copy distasteful and sleazy—especially "all those long copy sales letters on the Web" as one of my readers puts it.

Again, this is a pretty silly attitude when you think about it.

The longer the copy, the more information you are given about the product.

Is there something inherently unethical or inappropriate about giving prospects more information with which to make an intelligent buying decision?

Of course not.

But the real question for you as an entrepreneur is: despite direct marketing's less-than-sterling reputation in the minds of some consumers, should you use it to sell your product online and offline?

The answer is easy: unequivocally, yes.

Fortunately for us, the number of consumers who respond to direct response marketing is enough to give us highly profitable promotions.

So direct marketing remains an extremely effective method of selling merchandise and services.

22

Work Smarter–and Harder.

Business gurus are fond of saying, "Work smarter–not harder."

But I don't know...I think there is something to be said for hard work.

Assuming you and I work equally smart, I'd think whichever one of us worked the hardest would come out ahead.

Hard work is good for what ails you.

When your business or job isn't going the way you want it to, buckle down and redouble your efforts.

You'll be more productive, and at least some of your extra efforts will be rewarded–and hard work will have saved the day.

Goethe wrote, "Whoever strenuously endeavors, him we can rescue."

Combine hard work with persistence–never giving up–and the odds of you getting the result you want increase geometrically.

Ironically, a lot of people who work hard like to pretend that they don't.

A famous Internet marketer, in promoting his programs, boasts about how you can make a six figure income in Internet marketing with hardly any work.

But I happen to know that this guy works at least 12 hours a day, 6 days a week—and often late into the night.

A famous copywriter is pictured lounging in his pool in a magazine profile of him.

Yet he seems to be continually at his PC banging out successful ad after successful ad for his clients.

Most things that are worth having or achieving require hard work. If they were easy, everyone would have them.

Hard work alone does not guarantee success. You also have to work smart, of course.

But if you are not willing to put your nose to the grindstone, your chances of failure are large indeed.

Business or career floundering? Not where you want it to be?

Work twice as hard. You may get twice the results.

23

Maybe You Should Write a Book

To promote herself and her business, JL, one of my subscribers, wants to write a book.

But she isn't quite sure about how to get her book published and into print.

"It feels like getting a book published is challenging," she writes. "Would it not be easier to skip all the details and self-publish?"

Other Direct Response Letter subscribers with the desire to write a book and get it published have asked me the same question over the years.

"What's better?" an interviewer on an Internet radio show asked me, "Self-publishing or traditional publishing?"

It's the wrong question.

Self-publishing is not inherently better than mainstream publishing—nor is the reverse true.

Rather, there are 3 basic publishing options available to you—traditional publishing, self-publishing, and electronic publishing.

And the choice of which is right for you depends on your reasons for wanting to write and publish a book in the first place.

>> Option #1—Traditional publishing.

Of the 3 publishing options, selling your book to a mainstream book publishing company is the most prestigious.

Therefore, when you want to write a book to help establish you as a recognized expert in your field, traditional publishing is often the best option.

In the financial publishing industry, most stock market newsletter editors write at least one book for a mainstream publishing house.

Reason: being an author adds to their credibility, helping them sell subscriptions to their advisory letters.

>> Option 2—Self-publishing a physical book.

Self-publishing your book as a printed paperback or hardcover makes sense when you want to give away a lot of copies of your book as a marketing tool.

Professional speakers are a good example, because they typically send a free book, along with their sales materials, to every potential client.

Giving potential clients a copy of your book is an effective marketing tool. Information marketing pioneer Jeffrey Lant says "a book is a brochure that will never be thrown away."

The more professionally written, designed, and printed your self-published book, the more impressed your prospects will be.

Ideally, your self-published book should look no different than hardcover or trade paperback books from major publishers.

With self-publishing, your cost per copy is much less than buying your own book at the 50% author's discount off the cover price that you get from a regular publisher.

As a result, authors who give away a lot of copies of their books can save a lot of money with self-publishing.

If your goal is to sell copies of your book directly—whether through mail-order magazine ads, the Internet, or at the back of the room during speaking gigs—self-publishing gives you a higher profit margin.

>> Option 3—Publishing your book as an e-book.

Publishing your book as a downloadable PDF file—known as an "e-book"—is the clear choice when you want to: (a) sell your book on the Internet and (b) maximize your profits from its publication and sale.

Why are e-books so profitable? Two main reasons.

First, with an e-book, you can charge more money for less content than with a regular book.

Most traditionally published business books today are at least 200 pages—around 80,000 words—selling for at least $15 in trade paperback or $20 in hardcover.

For an e-book, you can charge anywhere from $29 to $49 per copy...more if the book is on a specialized topic.

And although length varies, a $29 e-book can be only 50 pages—about 15,000 words.

That means it costs as much as or more than a hardcover or paperback book while containing only one-fifth the text.

So it takes less writing time to produce an e-book than a regular book.

With an e-book, you deliver it to the buyer over the Internet as an electronic PDF file.

You can also format your e-book so Amazon can sell a Kindle version. My latest book had Kindle sales of over $9,000 last year.

With an e-book, there is no printing, storage, fulfillment, or shipping costs, so your profit margin on each sale is extremely high.

By comparison, authors who publish with mainstream publishers get a royalty averaging 10% or less of the book's cover price.

The margin in self-publishing physical books is usually 50% give or take 10%. But with e-books, the margin can be close to 100%.

24

Getting Started in Internet Marketing

When you hear about all the folks who are making thousands of dollars a week in passive income selling information products on the Internet...and "working" only a few hours a day...

...it's very tempting to want to chuck what you are doing and jump on the bandwagon.

But before you take the leap, it pays to think about whether Internet marketing is right for you.

On the surface, Internet information marketing sounds like everybody should be doing it.

Of course, if that happened, who would fix your car...or trim your hedges...or prepare your tax returns?

But not everybody is going to go into Internet marketing, of course—as tempting and attractive as it sounds.

Should you? Who else should? Who shouldn't?

To begin with, what you are selling as an Internet information marketer is useful knowledge on a specialized topic.

Therefore, if you already possess this specialized knowledge, you are in an advantageous position.

According to Gary North, most people in fact do have some specialized knowledge they can turn into a business.

"You possess a lot more knowledge than you think," says Gary. "In many cases, that knowledge is valuable to those who don't possess it."

If it's not immediately obvious to you what specialized knowledge you possess that other people would pay for, stop and take a personal inventory.

On a sheet of paper, list everything you know. Include your formal education...degrees...job history...skills...hobbies...and interests.

One or more of the items on your list most likely can be the basis of a profitable Internet information marketing business.

Are you articulate? If you can express yourself well in writing or orally, that also positions you for success in the Internet information marketing business.

You do not have to be a brilliant orator or a great writer. You just need the ability to express yourself clearly and concisely in a pleasing manner that people enjoy reading.

The next thing that gives you an advantage in the Internet marketing business is a strong desire to make more money than you are now making.

Money is important, because there are a lot of people who write and publish stuff (blogs, articles, poems, books, fiction) with little or no concern about money.

These dilettantes (and I am using the word in its literal meaning, not as a pejorative) post their stuff on the Web and give it away for free.

Their reward is sharing and knowing that people are reading or looking at their work

But putting up a Website and posting content to it is easy. Getting people to pay you for it is a bit more of a challenge—and requires a lot more work than just giving it away online.

An interest in making money from your intellectual property will give you the impetus and motivation to do the extra work it takes to create and sell information products online—a process I teach in my Internet Marketing Retirement Program: www.theinternetmarketingretirementplan.com

Have you studied copywriting? You do not need to be a good copywriter to have a successful Internet marketing business.

But you do need the ability to know whether a promotion written for you by a freelance copywriter is any good, so you can tell the writer how you want it fixed.

If you are a good copywriter, that's a bonus, because hiring top copywriters for landing pages and other sales copy is expensive—and by doing it yourself, you can avoid their fees.

Do you read marketing blogs and articles? If so, you have yet another advantage, because the key to success in Internet marketing is the marketing, not the content creation.

Quality content is important. But the people who make serious money online do so because they are good marketers, not because they are good writers or speakers.

Many people who love to write or speak are enamored with the "creative" part of communication, but aren't good at the business side of things. If you go into Internet marketing, you will have to pay more attention to the business side.

In particular, you need to know the numbers of Internet marketing and what you can realistically expect in terms of results from your promotions.

You do not need to have an aptitude for math, since the arithmetic of Internet marketing return on investment (ROI) is very simple and can be handled with a pocket calculator.

But you do need to be conscious of revenue coming in and money going out to cover expenses. Starting and running an Internet marketing business does not cost a lot of money, but the cost is not zero.

The one thing you absolutely do not need to start your own Internet marketing information business is knowledge of computers or technical ability of any kind.

The 3 most important skills for an Internet marketer to possess are: (1) marketing, (2) copywriting, and (3) communication (the ability to create content in writing and orally).

I advise Internet marketers to outsource all technical tasks such as setting up their computer, installing their e-commerce software, broadcasting e-mail marketing messages, maintaining their subscriber list, graphic design of e-books, video editing, and designing landing pages and Websites.

You can get people, both in the U.S. and especially overseas, to handle all these tasks at dirt-cheap prices. Go on Websites such as www.elance.com and www.rentacoder.com and you can easily find all the help you need, at prices so low they will astonish you.

Even if you can do the technical stuff, I advise you not to. That's right. Throw away your copy of Front Page or Dream Weaver—and hire someone else to design that landing page. Why?

With the limited amount of hours available for work each day, you need to spend your time on tasks that give you maximum return on time invested (ROTI).

The tasks with the highest ROTI revolve around thinking about your business and planning new products and marketing campaigns.

The technical stuff has the lowest ROTI. To be frank, it's a waste of your valuable time.

And the less efficient you are in running your Internet business, the more difficult achieving the "Internet marketing lifestyle"—making a six-figure passive income working only a few hours a day—will be to achieve.

To summarize, ask yourself:

>> Do I have useful knowledge of a specialized topic that people will pay for?

>>Can I express myself clearly orally and in writing?

>> Do I have a desire to earn more money from what I know?

>>Can I develop some skill in copywriting?

>> Do I understand the fundamentals of Internet marketing?

The more "yes" answers you gave, the better equipped you are to turn your knowledge into dollars.

25

Are You Ready for the Worst?

No one expects bad things—and by bad, I mean catastrophically bad—to happen to them.

Yet terrible tragedies happen to people who didn't expect them every day of the year.

You can't take a vaccine to immunize yourself against ill fortune.

But you can prepare for disasters before they happen.

That way, when they strike, you—and your family—will survive...with the minimum hardship possible.

In particular, here are 5 things I think you should do now to protect yourself against future problems and headaches:

1. Become financially secure.

Money can protect you against many disasters, and make many others easier to bear.

How much wealth should you strive to accumulate?

I recommend a goal of $2 million in liquid assets.

Reason: $2 million invested at 10% annual return produces an income of $200,000.

If a catastrophic illness or other crisis prevents you from working, you can just live off your investments.

And if your business fails or your career derails, you likewise can live off your investment income.

2. Buy life insurance.

Until you accumulate the $2 million, you need to leave an estate big enough to ensure a comfortable life for your family—preferably without forcing your spouse to sell the house and make the kids move.

Although a $2 million estate would be ideal, your spouse can probably get by nicely even with a million dollars in term life insurance on you.

Tip: buy this life insurance while you are young, before you have a serious illness.

Should you get sick, and then decide to get life insurance, the cost will be prohibitive.

3. Buy health insurance.

More than 46 million Americans do not have health insurance.

They are gambling their family's entire financial future.

One serious illness can quickly wipe out your life savings.

Get health insurance now. If you can't afford a private policy, join a group that offers discount coverage to members.

Tip: buy your insurance first. Then select doctors from the HMO's list of approved physicians.

That way, your doctor visits are covered by your plan, greatly reducing your health care costs.

4. Create sources of passive income.

What happens if you injure your back...or get a debilitating illness...and can't work?

Disability payments are often limited.

A better idea is to start creating sources of passive income now–sources that make money for you without you working.

One idea: investment real estate–rental properties.

Another: start an Internet marketing business that generates thousands of dollars in weekly revenues without any activity on your part.

Here's a Website where I discuss how you can make a six-figure passive income online with your own Internet marketing business:

www.theinternetmarketingretirementplan.com

5. Live for the moment.

This may seem contrary to the idea of "prepare for the future."

But it's really not.

When I was young, my father did not earn a high income, and constantly worried about money.

Yet my mother "forced" him to take at least one nice week-long vacation a year.

By some standards, these were far from "luxury" vacations–although they were very nice–but the cost certainly made him nervous.

Eventually, my father became ill from a cancer that would cause his death at a too-early age.

But by then, both he and my mother had a lifetime of great memories from their travels all over the globe with family and friends.

Had he waited until retirement, they wouldn't have shared those memories...because he died before he was able to quit working.

26

Be Happy With Who You Are

I've never been happy with who I am.

In fact, I feel quite guilty about it.

Let me explain...

I'm a bookworm...a bibliophile...a "bookaholic."

I am most content and fulfilled when I am sitting alone in my office, clicking away at the keyboard—writing copy for my clients or my own Internet marketing business—or articles and books for my publishers.

After a typical 12-hour day at the PC, I want nothing more than to sit on the couch—and read a book.

I don't play sports—or watch it on TV. No golf...no tennis...no bridge.

I don't garden...or do handyman stuff around the house...or have any discernible hobby—other than reading.

I love my kids, and enjoy spending time with my family...but I never voluntarily socialize with friends or relatives unless my wife pushes me to do so.

It seems to me that this makes me a narrow, limited person...hence the guilt and shame.

"It's not that I don't like people," writes NPR's book critic Maureen Corrigan. "It's just that when I'm in the company of others—even my nearest and dearest—there always comes a moment when I'd rather be reading a book."

As a bookaholic, I've developed another trait many consider odd: my preference for bad weather.

Gray, cold, rainy days make me happy.

While warm, cloudless days with sunshine make me depressed.

Why?

Because when it's cold and gray, I can stay inside...and read or write.

But when it's a nice day, I'm expected to participate in outdoor activities that I enjoy far less.

"My favorite kind of day is a cold, dreary, gusty, sleety day, when I can sit at my typewriter or word processor in peace and security," wrote the late Isaac Asimov.

"A perfect day fills me with the nameless dread (usually fulfilled) that Robyn [Asimov's daughter] will come to me, clapping her little hands in excitement, and say, 'Let's take a walk in the park. I want to go to the zoo.'

"Of course, I go, because I love her, but I tell you I leave my heart behind, stuck in the typewriter keys."

At this point in my life, I've spent over half a century feeling guilty over who I am—a prolific workaholic writer—what I like, and what I want to do: spend my life with words, information, and ideas.

Have you, like me, ever felt that you were letting people down by not being the type of person you think others expect you to be?

Well, I'm going to suggest that you join me now— and together, we let go of our guilt.

Let's embrace who we are, rather than reject it.

In the original "Nutty Professor" movie, Jerry Lewis says: "If you don't love yourself, how do you expect others to?"

"Be a real person," advises my friend, Internet marketing guru Fred Gleeck. "People are sick of phonies. Be who you really are and don't worry if some people don't like you. For those who don't, there are plenty who will LOVE you for being yourself."

Listen: I don't know why I am so addicted to books and the printed word.

I just can't help it. Nothing comes close to engaging my admittedly limited intellect the way writing does.

But now, I don't care–or feel bad about it–anymore.

That's the way I am, and after 56 years of living, now I am at peace with it.

I hope you can be at peace with who–and what–you are, as well.

Because–to quote another actor, Vince Vaughn in "Dodgeball"–"you're perfect just the way you are."

27

Make a Back-Up Plan

In the movie "Armageddon," a giant asteroid is hurtling toward Earth, and when it hits, the impact will annihilate everything on the planet.

The government's solution?

Send a team of drilling experts up into outer space to land on the asteroid.

Their mission: drill a deep hole into its core, drop an atom bomb down the hole, and detonate it, blowing the asteroid to smithereens.

Only problem is, Bruce Willis, the leader of the drill team, thinks the chances of success are slim.

"What's your back-up plan?" he asks Billy Bob Thorton, his NASA liaison.

"Back-up plan?" Thorton says. "There's no back-up plan. This is the only plan we have."

Most of us are like Billy Bob, in that—in business, career, and life—we have no back- up plan.

But we should.

None of these guys had a back-up plan:

** AH went into computer programming in the 1980s when it was a booming profession, and was quickly earning a six-figure salary. Within a few years, his job got outsourced to India, and the salary he was offered for another IT job was less than half his current pay.

** PM worked as a manager for a local family-owned business. One day the boss called him in and said: "Times are tough, and to keep you, I have to reduce your salary by 40%. I know you'll understand." PM quit the next day.

** HR had a comfortable job as a hospital administrator until he was downsized. To his amazement, he found himself unqualified for any other work...and after months of fruitless job searching, had to raise cash to live on by selling off his prized collection of antiquarian books.

** LL earned a decent living as a woodworker. But the constant exposure to sawdust and varnish was making him sick, to the point where he could not continue to earn a living in the only profession he was trained for.

** BD spent months developing a piece of software that was going to revolutionize the Internet marketing world and make him rich in the process. Last month, Google announced they were offering virtually the same software–for free.

Most of us think bad things can never happen...or that they only happen to "the other guy."

But what happens when we become "the other guy"?

You–and I–need a "back-up plan."

This could be:

1. Buy income-producing real estate and other appreciating assets. Invest prudently and build your net worth to the point where you can live off your real estate and other investments.

2. Learn a second skill or profession. LL learned copywriting and today earns $400,000 a year as a freelance copywriter.

3. Create and sell a line of products–anything from candles and perfume to exercise videos and how-to books.

4. Collect a sizeable inheritance that will enable you to live the life of a gentleman or lady of leisure.

5. Marry a spouse with a good income who will support you in the style to which you have become accustomed.

Of these options, my own back-up plan is #3 (mainly because #4 and #5 didn't pan out).

About 18 months ago, I began to think, "What if something happens to me so that I am unable to continue making a living as a freelance writer?"

So I started my own Internet marketing business creating and selling information products–e-books, audios, and videos–online.

That was a year and a half ago.

Today, my little Internet marketing business generates a steady $4,000 to $4,500 a week in income for me...and yet I spend only an hour or two a week on it!

That comes out to over $200,000 a year–which means I never have to work again a day in my life if I don't want to.

Listen: you need a back-up plan...and you can choose any of the 5 listed above.

28

Become an Indispensable Expert

Are you absolutely indispensable...?

...to your clients...customers...employer...or anyone else you want to buy what you are selling?

Most people are not. Not by a long shot.

These very same people complain bitterly when the client haggles over their price quote...or the customer chooses another vendor...or the boss passes them over for promotion.

Yet, they do nothing to make themselves indispensable—or to offer a skill, expertise, knowledge, product, or service the buyer cannot do without.

But now you can.

And when you are indispensable, you are always in demand.

Since you are always in demand, you can always earn a good income.

Therefore, becoming indispensable gives you a level of financial security very few workers enjoy.

The most important piece of advice I ever got on becoming indispensable was given to me by PS, a wealthy investor and mining consultant who made his fortune in gold.

"Become an expert in something," PS told me. "If you know something–something that other people don't know, but need or want to know–you will always live well."

PS is right.

When you know something better than other people...and can offer them some valuable and unique knowledge or expertise–you are in the driver's seat.

OK. So how do you become an indispensable expert?

Here are the 5 steps:

** First, take a personal inventory.

What have you done in your life?

What are you passionate about?

What do you do well?

What do you have an aptitude for?

** Second, based on your personal inventory, select the general area in which you want to become an expert.

Examples: real estate...parenting...sex...digital photography...investments...computers...nutrition.

** Third, narrow the niche.

There are too many established experts in the general areas listed above for you to compete head on.

So find a segment of the topic or market, and own it.

AS, a former real estate agent, wants to become a real estate guru.

But there are already too many people competing in "real estate."

We found through a Web search that tons of people online are searching the key phrase "lake house" online.

AS owns a lake house.

Guess what?

She is launching a site with content and products for people who own—or want to buy—lakefront property.

** Fourth, dominate your niche.

How?

Take on more projects or clients in that niche.

Attend the industry trade shows.

Read the trade publications religiously.

Write articles for the leading trade publication in your niche.

Even better, become a columnist.

** Fifth, monetize your expertise.

Make sure your niche is one where people or organizations will pay handsome fees to gain access to your expertise.

Create products and services you can market to those people at a profit.

29

Do You Want to be Rich?

Is being rich the most important thing in the world to you?

It's not to me.

Now, don't get me wrong.

I like having money...and I do think it's important.

Ted Nicholas and others have noted that there are 4 factors necessary for a happy and successful life.

They are:

1–Money.

2–Enjoyable, meaningful work.

3–Love (family, relationships).

4–Health.

I've always thought that health is the overriding component of a happy and successful life.

If you are in poor health, it's difficult to enjoy the money, work, friends, and family to their fullest.

As for #3, I am a family guy. My wife and I dote on our kids.

But as important as relationships are, one can argue that it is the most dispensable of the 4 happiness factors.

After all, there seem to be many people who get along in this life at least reasonably well without children, spouse, lovers, and friends.

(Or maybe they're not happy but just hide it well.)

Lots of people think the solution to their unhappiness is money: if only they had money, all their problems would go away.

Rich people know that money alone is no assurance of a happy or problem-free life.

That being said, the older I get, the more I appreciate the important of money.

Money does bring you some very valuable advantages. These include:

>>Power...Bill Gates can do more good in the world than I can because he has a $37 billion charitable foundation. Money enhances your ability to help others.

>>Security...when you attain financial independence, your money worries are gone for good, an enviable position to be in. Millions of Americans worry about money.

>>Comfort...money insulates you from hunger and homelessness, and ensures access to basic services such as heat, electricity, potable water, and health care—stuff we take for granted but millions worldwide lack.

>>Luxury...for those who desire it, wealth allows you to indulge yourself, whether living in a mansion on the ocean, driving a Porsche, or dining on the finest caviar.

>>Freedom...with enough money, you choose what you do, where and when you do it, and who you do it with...and never have to work at a job you hate because you need the cash.

However, for me, it's not enough to make a lot of money.

I have to earn my money doing something I love–in other words, only the combination of #1 (money) and #2 (rewarding work) above works for me.

Are you like me?

I suspect that if you are a subscriber to this e-newsletter, you are.

Your interests revolve around many of the same things that stimulate me.

These include books... reading... writing... marketing... communication... small business... information marketing... the Internet... the written word.

For you, the trick is to find the intersection of your interests and the needs of the marketplace. Simply making a lot of money by any means available won't do it for you.

So...how can you find a niche that gives you a great income, enjoyment, and deep satisfaction?

Here's where to start:

1–Your experience...what you have done.

2–Your interests...what stimulates you, turns you on, engages your mind, body, and spirit...in other words, your passions.

3–Your education...not just your college major, but any special skills, trades, technology, processes, or other specialized knowledge you've learned.

4–Your aptitudes...what you are good at and like to do.

5–Your expertise...what you know that others will pay money to learn from you.

Of course, if you only care about money, and not what you have to do to accumulate it, your path is easier.

Then you can be an orthodontist, lawyer, investment banker, or any other profession that's highly paid.

But if not, you won't be happy until you find, as I have, a way to turn your interests and passions–such as reading, writing, or marketing–into a product or service people want and will pay for.

30

Overcoming Job Burnout

Are you suffering from job burnout?

Losing the enthusiasm, joy, and excitement about writing, marketing, or whatever it is you do?

Are you bored... fatigued... depressed... stressed... overworked... anxious... suffering from low self-esteem...or having difficulty concentrating or giving customers your best?

Job burnout is what happened to my friend KJ, a successful freelance copywriter.

"After a few years of going all out, my drive started to slip away," writes KJ. "I started getting tired and burned out."

KJ's solution?

She developed a second income stream...so she didn't have to write copy for clients under deadline all the time.

KJ chose as her second income stream to start an Internet marketing business.

"Before I fully understood why, I was walking away from some of my clients and moving towards writing for my own products," she says.

Not only did this give KJ a second source of income—freeing her from having to constantly serve clients and work on their timetable...

But it also gave her renewed enthusiasm for her freelance copywriting business...a side result that was somewhat unexpected.

"Now that I've cut back on my freelance clients, I'm excited about the work again," KJ says. "The fire has returned."

KJ discovered that adding more variety to her working day—not just working for a boss or clients but also selling her own products—was just the thing she needed to revitalize her passion for writing.

Having a second stream of income has another benefit: when you do not depend on your job for money, work becomes optional, not mandatory—and your attitude often improves as a result.

Here are some additional tips to help you avoid job burnout:

>> Take on new projects...for instance, if you are interested in online marketing and want to learn more about it, ask your boss if you can work on optimizing your company's Website for search engines or manage a pay-per-click ad campaign.

>> Become more active in your own field ...sometimes, decades of working in the same profession can cause you to lose your sense of wonder and intellectual engagement. The cure may be to dive right back in with renewed vigor, like becoming involved in the local chapter of your professional association or writing an article for your industry trade publication.

>> Find intellectual stimulation outside of work...especially for workaholics, hobbies can be a tonic for burnout. You can take up chess, study a foreign language, paint, sculpt, snowboard, spelunk, or learn to play a new instrument (anybody out there have a used bass saxophone they want to sell me cheap?).

>> Update your resume...and quietly put some feelers out for a job search. Even if you don't actually make a move, just knowing that you are valuable and wanted can lift you out of the doldrums.

>> Revert to the passions of your youth...doing something you did when you were younger but don't do now—whether playing basketball or watching "I Love Lucy" reruns—can have a psychologically rejuvenating effect.

Finally, exercise regularly. Especially if you have a desk job like copywriting or management, the break in your sedentary routine can refresh and energize you on a daily basis.

31

SWL + SWNL = SW

Customer service books and seminars teach us that "the customer is always right."

That would mean every customer is right–all the time.

But clearly, that can't be the case.

A case in point: in the survey I sent out to you guys a few weeks ago, many of the responses I received were diametrically opposed.

For instance, when I asked for feedback on my e-zine, "The Direct Response Letter," subscriber EP complained that it was too short.

"Make your content messages more meaty instead of barely useful little snippets of other people's information," EP complained in a long, negative e-mail.

That same day, HM, another subscriber, also sent me an e-mail. But her take on my e-mail messages was quite different than EP's.

"I love that the topics are short, and I love your e-zine," said HM. "It's one I read from top to bottom every time it arrives."

So, if the customer is always right, which customer is right here–EP or HM?

Do I make my e-mails longer like EP requested? Or keep them short and pithy to please HM?

The answer, of course, is that both EP and HM know what's right for them...and what they want.

Therefore, I have to be guided by a success formula created by my good friend, motivational speaker Dr. Rob Gilbert.

Rob's formula is: SWL + SWL = SW.

Translation:

>> Some people will like (you, your product, your service).

>> Some people won't like (you, your product, your service).

>> So what?

In other words: you can't please all of the people all of the time...and you shouldn't even try.

What does this mean for you and your business?

It means you should create products, publications, services, and content that reflect who you are and what you do best.

When you do this, some people will like your products, publications, services, and content.

These folks are your best prospects...your most loyal readers...your most profitable customers...your diamond clients.

Give them more of what they like, and you will be successful.

On the other hand, some people will not like your products, publications, services, and content.

They are not good prospects for what you are selling. And they never will be, because if you change to please them, you will cease delivering what your loyal customers come to you for...and they will start buying from your competitor.

Remember: SWL + SWL = SW.

Some will like you. Some will not like you.

So what?

Embrace those who like you and cater to these customers to make them more loyal, serve them better, and get them to buy more.

As for those who do not like you, let them go.

You can't please everybody, and you shouldn't even try.

32

Don't Hide Behind E-Mail

I've done it...and I bet you have, too.

I'm talking about sending an e-mail to someone just to avoid talking with them on the telephone.

The excuse I make is that the other person and I are both busy—and communicating by e-mail is more efficient and convenient.

As a result of this insidious habit of using the Internet to duck personal one-on-one contact, e-mail has just about made regular business letters obsolete—and is threatening to do the same to face-to-face meetings and telephone calls.

But there are some things e-mails aren't good for— and one of them is conveying emotion.

The mood or emotion of the sender is so difficult to accurately interpret, we use "emoticons" to get them across.

Like this one to communicate that our comment is tongue-in-cheek, friendly, or light-hearted. ☺

How do you avoid the e-mail trap...and build a closer relationship with your important friends, colleagues, and customers?

Two simple words: "client contact."

I have a big sign posted on the wall in my office. In big, boldface letters are just two words: "CLIENT CONTACT."

The sign reminds me that I should reach out to people—my subscribers, readers, prospects, clients, colleagues, friends, and even relatives—more often with a phone call or in person, and less often with e-mail.

If you're introverted, pressed for time, or just not a people person, start small like I did.

Ever since posting the "Client Contact" sign on my wall, I have used it as a reminder to proactively phone at least one person every day—even when there is not a pressing matter to discuss or an urgent reason to do so.

I advise you to, as an experiment, do the same: make and post a big sign that says "CLIENT CONTACT" near your desk.

Then meet in person...or call on the phone ...at least one client, prospect, colleague, or associate a day—in particular, someone you don't HAVE to call but should.

I think you will, within a few weeks, notice an immediate improvement in both your relationships with people...and your attitude towards them.

33

Six Steps to a More Successful Life

Why do some people make millions while others struggle to pay their monthly credit card bills?

Why are some people rich and powerful while others look on in envy and awe?

Why do people who seem no smarter or better than you or I lead lives of seeming ease and affluence...while others are mired in worry and debt?

I am confident I have the answer...as well as a way for you to become happier and more fulfilled in your life—starting almost immediately.

Let me explain...

As I see it, there are 6 factors responsible for any individual's success or lack thereof, especially in business and wealth building.

They are:

>> Aptitude...some people gravitate towards activities that make money (e.g., they are interested in investing or business)—while others are naturally attracted to fields that are less lucrative (e.g., poetry, pottery).

>> Hard work...some people are willing to put in grueling hours to achieve great wealth and material abundance. Others are not willing to sacrifice their hours for dollars, and would rather spend their time in other ways, from playing golf to going camping with their kids.

>> Luck...no matter how much of a technical genius or savvy businessman Bill Gates is, a lot of his success was largely the result of being in the right place at the right time.

>> Perseverance...many rich and successful people got that way simply because they persisted vs. the vast majority who give up at the first roadblock or failure.

>> Brains...being smart–either in the classic I.Q. smart or street smarts–is a decided advantage. And despite what our Constitution says, not all of us are born equal in this regard.

>> Talent...no matter how much I want it or how much I train, there is no chance on Earth of me becoming the next American Idol–or even runner-up.

All of these factors obviously have a great effect on the course of your life.

But of these, I believe aptitude is the most important–and unfortunately, the one least under our control.

I mean: you like what you like.

You read about those guys on Wall Street with their million-dollar bonuses. And maybe you turn green with envy.

But in your mind you know–and say to yourself– "Hey, that ain't for me."

The comforting old saying motivational speakers love to spout is that "if you pursue your passion, the money will come."

Sadly, this often isn't true.

My friend SB pursued his passion as a poet for over 40 years.

He had dozens of his poems published in magazines.

But he is neither rich nor famous–although I believe (but don't know for certain) that SB is pretty happy.

So, how can you find more success, peace, and happiness in your life?

You have to make a decision.

The decision is whether to pursue your passion and enjoy it and be at peace with that path in life...even if you never make much money doing it.

Or, you can decide that your primary goal is money.

You want to be rich, and you are willing to do whatever it takes to make that happen–reasoning that once you are rich, then you can afford to indulge in your passions.

For me, it wasn't much of a choice.

Don't get me wrong: I like money. But being rich was never that important to me, especially when I was younger.

My passion was writing, and I decided that, if I could make a decent living doing what I love–writing–in any form, I would be happy.

That worked out for me: I've been a writer for nearly 30 years, and I can't imagine doing anything else.

Action step: sit down and write out a description of your ideal day.

If living that ideal life would make you happy, make a plan for its achievement.

34

Five Steps to Making Your Writing Less Stuffy

Here are a few quick writing tips that can make your copy leaner, less stuffy, and more concise:

1—Get rid of "that."

Nine times out of ten, the word "that" can be profitably eliminated from your sentence.

Original: "Here are the key metrics that Web analysts measure."

Better: "Here are the key metrics Web analysts measure."

2—Do not invoke the future tense unless it is needed.

Original: "Optimizing your Website will increase traffic."

Better: "Optimizing your Website increases traffic."

3—Do not capitalize words to emphasize their importance.

Original: "It is the policy of the Company to provide up to 10 paid Sick Days."

Better: "It is the policy of the company to provide up to 10 paid sick days."

4—Say what you have to say in the fewest words possible.

Original: "He was driving at an excessive rate of speed."

Better: "He was driving too fast."

5—Avoid dangling modifiers.

Wrong: "As a policyholder, I want you to know that you can reduce your premiums by 50% this year."

Correct: "As a policyholder, you can reduce your premiums by 50% this year."

35

Seven Reasons Most Writers Don't Make Much Money

Most of the writers I know—and I know a truckload of them—don't make much money.

Here are 7 factors that hold writers back from earning six-figure incomes...and achieving a seven-figure net worth...and one good way to avoid each:

1—A Poverty Mentality.

Some writers have a misguided romantic notion about toiling in obscurity for a pittance.

Understand that there is nothing noble, romantic, or the least bit charming about being poor.

Money is not the root of evil.

But lack of money—poverty—causes many of the world's ills.

2—Not Valuing Their Time.

What is the dollar value of your time per hour?

If a specific dollar figure did not leap immediately to mind, then you don't really value your time.

And if you don't value your time, then your time has no value.

3—Volunteer Mania.

Stay away from volunteering for groups or committees—it saps energy and wastes time that could be spent writing.

Exceptions? Of course.

But be aware that for every hour you do fun or meaningful volunteer work, you lose an hour of billable writing time.

4–The Commodity Trap.

Don't be "just another writer"...churning out books, articles, and stories on anything and everything someone will pay you for.

Instead, specialize.

Be the leader in your writing niche.

William Novak is the top ghostwriter.

Carline Anglade Cole is one of the top nutritional supplement writers.

Dick Sanders is a top magalog writer.

Herschell Gordon Lewis is tops in collectibles.

You get the idea.

5–Haggling Over Nickels and Dimes.

Too many writers haggle over nickels and dimes– and as a result, earn only nickels and dimes.

Don't work for markets that pay $100 a project and fight with the editor until she gives in and raises your fee to $110.

Instead, write for markets that routinely pay $1,000 a project.

6–No Passive Income.

Most writers are like dentists: unless you're drilling and filling, you're not billing.

To get rich without working yourself to death, develop sources of passive income: real estate, investments, royalties, an Internet marketing business.

7–Lack of Self Promotion.

You may find selling distasteful, but as my colleague JH once said, "Everybody has to sell–at least part of the time."

All you produce is words and ideas, and there are lots of those being created every day–and given away freely online.

You must show your clients and customers how your writing services or written products can help them save or make money...save time...succeed in business...gain financial security...or otherwise benefit them in their personal or business life.

36

Avoid This Common Writing Mistake

The most common writing mistake...

...is not possessing wide knowledge–and deep understanding–of the subject you are writing about.

You might have strong writing skills.

But if you lack mastery of your topic, your writing will be vague, unfocused, and have little value, credibility, and authority.

To prevent this error, use the following 4-step formula for more powerful writing:

1–Accumulate knowledge.

The late Paul Sarnoff, a successful author and newsletter editor, said: "If you are an expert in something, you will never go hungry."

Before you can write, you need to have something to write about.

This means acquiring extensive knowledge and deep understanding–through a combination of research and experience–of a subject people will pay to learn.

2–Organize your content.

What's the best way to present your subject? Is it a process with definite sequential steps that must be performed in a specific order?

Find a logical organizational scheme that fits the subject matter; e.g., a book on vitamins and minerals could present topics in alphabetical order, starting with vitamin A and ending with zinc.

3—Teach your subject.

Use illustrations, stories, examples, case studies, photos, diagrams, tables, analogies, metaphors, comparisons—whatever it takes to make your subject clear to the reader.

Give plenty of examples, worksheets, resources, and model documents the reader can copy so he does not have to reinvent the wheel.

4—Polish your prose.

Here's where your writing skill comes into play. When style is not dictated by the client, publisher, or format, write in a natural, conversational style—like one friend talking to another, or a patient teacher looking over the reader's shoulders.

Use small words, short sentences, and short paragraphs. Avoid jargon. Write in plain simple English.

37

Live Below Your Means

A favorite ploy of some who sell "get rich quick" in copywriting or Internet marketing...

...is to boast about the luxury cars and other expensive toys they have bought—presumably with the money they made from the skill they are offering to teach you.

One, whom I am personally quite fond of and greatly admire, brags about his new $350,000 Rolls Royce.

Another sends us a photo of her with her new Jaguar.

A third describes the multi-million-dollar home he is having built.

Now, there's nothing wrong with wanting or having these possessions.

But if—like me—you don't care about the trappings of wealth...

...then not being extravagant in your spending can actually give you an advantage as a freelancer or entrepreneur.

The best business advice I ever got was from Florida freelance writer DK, who told me:

"Live below your means."

It is advice I have always followed...and I am glad I have done so.

You see, I'm a tightwad by nature. Not with others. But with myself.

Given the choice between dinner at a 4-star restaurant and plain old food...I'll take Denny's any time.

This year, for instance, I needed a new car.

Now, I can't afford a Rolls Royce.

But I can afford a Jag, a Lexus, a Benz, or most of the other luxury cars—and keep in mind, I always buy my cars for cash.

I never lease or loan.

In fact, I live a lifestyle that allows me to have no consumer debt of any kind—except mortgages on investment properties.

So what car did I settle on?

A new 2008 Toyota Prius Hybrid.

It cost me—including taxes—only $23,500.

I love driving it. Handles well. Looks great. Very sporty. Fits in small parking spaces.

Most important, it gets 45 miles per gallon.

Why do I advise that you live below your means—as DK and I do?

It's simple.

By living below your means, you remove unnecessary financial pressure from your life.

That way, you can make business decisions ...e.g., what clients or projects to take on...based on what you want to do—and not financial need.

When you live below your means, you can do what you want to do...when you want to do it...which to me is a recipe for a happy and rewarding life.

When you live way above your means, you become a slave to your possessions—working to pay for the toys you have—and buy the next ones.

That may be a good way for some people to live.

But not for me.

And maybe not for you.

Of course, it's your call.

38

Ten Bad Behaviors You Should Avoid

I know I am a crabby old man who is probably too easily annoyed.

But there are some things people do that irritate me so much I believe they may tick many other people off too.

For this reason, you may want to avoid committing these sins yourself, for fear of alienating your customers, business associates, and friends:

1–Do you constantly brag to others about how busy you are? It can rapidly become tiresome, irritating, and distasteful.

Barbara Ehrenreich calls this "the cult of busyness": the appearance of being busy as a status symbol. I advise you to avoid it. Get over yourself: You are not really that important.

2–Especially in the world of Internet marketing, the boasting of how successful one is has reached epic proportions.

It's nothing new. Decades ago, Joe Karbo in his Lazy Man's Way to Riches ads bragged about the cars, boats, and houses he owned

...and showed a picture of his Rolls Royce.

But if another marketing guru tells me about his beachfront mansion or shows a picture of his new Bentley on Facebook, I may barf in my Prius. Enough is enough.

3–Boasting of any kind is offensive to me and many others. It is just not necessary. People brag to make themselves feel

successful as well as superior to the listener. How is that good communication?

4–Stop shoving your latest gadgets in my face to show me how they work. I really don't care. If I did, I would buy one.

I do not own an iPhone, iPod, or iPad and have no desire to.

People think I am crazy, but there is a reason for my luddite behavior: Those devices enable mobility with productivity, but Iam not a mobile worker:

I work in my home office with a desktop PC and landline phone, and almost never travel. So the gadgets in my case are unnecessary. And I have no interest in your toys.

I'm also pretty indifferent to your new $2,500 barbecue that looks like the console from the U.S.S. Enterprise.

5–I wager that none of my readers do this, but just in case: Do not play your car stereo so loudly that people in other cars can hear it. You may be proud of your taste in music, but when driving, keep it inside the vehicle at all times.

6–On Facebook and other social networks, feel free to share interests and content. But don't make your posts thinly disguised sales pitches for your products or services. It is unseemly and violates social media etiquette as I understand it to be.

7–Another pet peeve: people who treat their personal opinion as fact. That the speed of light is 186,000 miles per second is a fact. That you think the U.S. should take action against the Syrian government is your opinion. Learn to recognize the difference.

8–Nitpicking is by and large an annoying habit. Let the little things go. Example: pointing out typos wherever you find them.

Note: I admit that opinions vary on this point. Some say God is in the details. Others say not to sweat the small stuff.

9–Correcting people does not endear you to them. My #1 rule in life is: do not give unsolicited advice. People think free advice is worth exactly what they paid for it: nothing.

10–Be less argumentative. Contentious people are not fun to be around. Be more easygoing. If you are chomping at the bit to prove yourself right and others wrong, ask yourself: why?

One other: don't wear a cowboy hat unless you are a cowboy.

39

Twenty-Five Secrets of Lasting Success

A few weeks ago, Bill R., a subscriber, wrote me the following e-mail:

"What advice would you give somebody starting out who wants to be a success—as a copywriter or just in life in general? What advice would you give to a son or a nephew graduating high school or college as they go into the world?

"I guess I am looking for the one thing that you think is most important to being successful or most important in life in general…or any words of wisdom that you have. What is the one thing about life that everybody should know to be happy?"

It's an intimidating request, because the older I get, the less I seem to know.

When Thomas Edison wrote that "we don't know one-millionth of one percent about anything," you can certainly apply that to me and success.

My own accomplishments are fairly modest. I earn a nice living, but I am not in the Donald Trump or the Michael Masterson league—or even close.

My family and I live a pretty ordinary life, in a pretty ordinary suburb.

I like to think I'm a good dad. But I am not sure my sons always agree. Other than my family and work, I don't have many other interests or activities (except reading).

So I am not confident that Bill is asking the right person for advice on how to achieve success in business and in life.

And yet he is not the first to ask me. I get dozens of similar requests a year from my readers.

So to satisfy Bill–and maybe you–here's what little I know about prospering and enjoying life.

Please keep in mind that my advice may not be right for you. It is merely what has worked–or not worked–for me:

1–Be yourself. Do not pretend to be someone or something you are not. Your uniqueness will appeal to a certain segment of the market. These folks become your best fans and customers.

2–Following your passion–doing what you love–does not guarantee financial success. But not doing what you love guarantees a life of boredom and unhappiness. The trick is to find a niche where your passions and interests intersect with the needs of the market.

3–Learn a financially valuable skill so you can command a decent salary or (if you are self employed) a respectable fee.

4–Those workers and service providers who command top dollar either: (a) perform a service that makes or saves their employer or client money or time, (b) have a skill for which the demand exceeds the supply, or (c) specialize in a narrow niche with little competition.

5–If you can earn a salary or generate a net income as a self-employed service professional or independent contractor of $200,000 a year or more, you won't get rich. But your life will be easier and you will be financially more secure than 95% of Americans.

6–Given the choice, have your children when you are young and possess the energy it takes to parent active youngsters.

7–Spend as much time as you can with your children when they are young and still want you, even if you must make sacrifices in your professional achievements to do so. This time passes quickly and once it's gone, it's gone for good.

8–Strive to achieve a liquid net worth of at least $2 million by age 50. You won't be rich, but again, you'll have more financial security than about 95% of Americans.

9–The best piece of financial advice I ever got was from Florida freelance writer David Kohn, who told me: "Live below your means." Doing so further enhances your financial security.

10–With your wealth, avoid buying material possessions that are unnecessary–especially luxuries that depreciate in value over time. Use your money to buy income-producing assets, assets that appreciate in value, or services that free up your time for other activities.

11–Avoid debt of any kind to the extent you are able. I have zero consumer debt except the mortgages on investment properties. Cars I buy for cash. If you have to get a loan or lease to drive a particular model car, you can't afford it.

12–If you lend money to friends or family, do it with the expectation that the money is really a gift rather than a loan, and do not expect to ever get the money back. If you are repaid, even in part, consider it found money.

13–Every day you wake up and everyone in your family is in good health, and you have food to eat and a decent place to live, you are ahead of the game.

14–When writers, Internet marketers, and entrepreneurs brag to you about how much money they make, divide the figure they give by three. As my colleague Fred Gleeck is fond of pointing out, the only numbers you can trust are your own.

15–Always in your business, under-promise and over-deliver. Give your customers not their money's worth, but more than they have a right to expect. Err on the side of being too generous rather than being too rigid or strict.

16–Before criticizing a supplier or vendor, say something positive–what you like about the work–first. The more insulted a vendor feels, the less motivated they become to serve you.

17–Do not allow yourself to be belittled, insulted, or demeaned verbally or in writing by others. When someone makes a snide or degrading comment, your reply should be: "What was your purpose in making that comment to me?" It will stop them in their tracks, and embarrass them so they never do it again to you.

18—Do not give people unsolicited advice.

19—To paraphrase Dan Kennedy, guard your time like the gold in Fort Knox. You can always make more money, but time lost or wasted is gone forever.

20—As long as a business or life decision does not involve risking the mortgage money, make it quickly. Successful people are able to make swift decisions and carry them out with speed.

21—The #1 difference between successful people and those less successful is that successful people act on their ideas. Ideas are a dime a dozen. Without action, ideas are worthless.

22—Do not think you must reinvent the wheel on every new product or business project. Most things have already been done before. All you need to do is add a twist or put your own spin on a product or service to create demand and make it profitable.

23—If you are successful, you can be arrogant and boastful. But why do it? Your bragging makes others who are less successful feel badly about themselves. What's the point of doing that? And don't refer to yourself as a genius or superstar in your marketing copy. If you were a genius, you wouldn't have to say it—instead others would be saying it and you could quote them.

24—Focus on your work—on creating valuable products, giving great service, going the extra mile for your customers–rather than how much money you want to make.

25–Start investing right away, when you are young. Do this early enough, and compounding can make you rich. Wait until you're 50 and 60, and you could find yourself in desperate straits. And diversify. Put 10% of your wealth in an investment that moves in opposition to the stock market, such as precious metals.

40

Work is More Fun Than Fun

In his book "Confessions of an Advertising Man," David Ogilvy quotes an old Scottish proverb about happiness:

"Be happy while you're living, for you're a long time dead."

The idea is that you should do everything in your power to be happy now, because tomorrow you might not be here.

Given that I am now beyond the sunny side of 50, the truth of this reality becomes clearer with each passing year.

I don't know the ultimate secret of lifetime happiness, as so many self-help writers and motivational speakers seem to.

But I'm pretty sure I know what makes millions of Americans unhappy.

It's their work.

"Walden" author Henry David Thoreau said, "Most men lead lives of quiet desperation."

I am convinced that Thoreau is right.

And the reason so many lead lives of quiet desperation is they work 40 to 50 hours a week at a job that they tolerate at best.

And at worst, they hate.

A 2007 survey from CareerBuilder.com confirmed that 84% of U.S. workers do not have their dream jobs, which most people define as "work that is fun."

For that reason, I have made it a priority–and I suggest you do the same–to make sure you have a job you not only like...but absolutely love: a job that is fun.

That's right.

It's not enough to like work.

You should ideally love it.

By that, I mean literally hop out of bed each morning, so eager to work that you can't wait to get into the office and turn on your PC (or do whatever it is you do).

I have been earning my living by writing for 30 years–and I still wake up early, happy that I get to come to this office, sit here alone listening to my music, and type 12 hours a day!

Of course, I don't love every aspect of my job: I don't like paperwork. And dealing with technical PC or Internet issues is pure misery for me (which is why I pay an assistant to handle these nuisances).

But as for the work itself...writing...I absolutely love it.

Noel Coward said: "Work is more fun than fun."

That is certainly the case for me.

I am in complete agreement on this subject with both Mr. Coward and my writing hero, Isaac Asimov, who said:

"I am so ill-rounded that the ten things I love to do are: write, write, write, write, write, write, write, write, write, and write. Oh, I do other things. I even like to do other things. But when asked for the ten things I love, that's it."

On a radio advice show the other day, the guest told listeners: "Find something you really love to do, and find a way to make money doing it."

If that's not the ultimate key to happiness, for me it is darn close to it–and just could be for you, too.

Should you somehow find a way to arrange to do what you love for your work...and earn a good living from it...then consider yourself blessed with good fortune.

"It's a privilege to be able to do what you love to do and be good at it," said guitar legend Les Paul.

"My hobby is my work, and my work is my hobby. That's the secret. There's no distinction."

41

How I Spend My Day

Subscriber AM recently wrote me:

"Hey Bob, your guru Mark Ford has already provided us with a description of his daily schedule. We would also be interested in knowing how you schedule your day."

I'm afraid my schedule is much less diverse and interesting than Mark's, though perhaps in its own way instructive:

I work 12 hours a day, 5 days a week, from 7am to 7pm EST Monday through Friday.

That's the ideal schedule, anyway.

Of course, there are the occasional unavoidable interruptions.

So to make up for lost time, I normally (but not always) put in 2-4 hours on Saturday.

Sundays I usually take off. And in really nice weather in the spring, I may leave an hour or two early on Friday evening to sit in the yard while the sun is still out and read the paper.

Of course, I do spend some weekends "working"– giving or taking seminars.

But those weekends are the exception, not the rule.

During the week, I devote the mornings to the tough work–writing copy for my clients.

I continue writing client copy after lunch for a few hours, until I lose steam.

The rest of my work day is spent on these tasks:

>> Managing my little Internet information marketing business, CTC Publishing.

>> Editing e-books written for CTC Publishing by my freelancers.

>> Writing my own books, articles, and columns.

>>Doing some blogging, social networking, and content syndication to promote my Internet business.

>> Routine correspondence with customers, readers, prospects, clients, colleagues.

>> Phone interviews with subject matter experts I must talk with to gather information for writing projects.

During my 12-hour stint in the office, I take a half hour off for lunch.

So...what can you take away from my work habits that can help you be more productive?

Here are 2 quick tips...

First, notice that I work a 12-hour day.

When a reporter asked the great Claude Hopkins why he earned twice as much as any other copywriter of his day, he answered that he worked twice as long.

One key to super-productivity is simply to put your nose to the grindstone, dedicate yourself to work, and get things done.

Motivational speakers and coaches implore us to work smarter, not harder.

But most of the really successful people I know work smarter *and* harder than their competitors.

The other tip is to break your work day into one hour increments and assign a different task to each hour.

This is particularly useful on days when you can't seem to get moving or motivated.

Just write out the schedule...and do for the hour what it says on the schedule.

AM also asked me about hobbies and travel, but there isn't much to tell here.

That's because another key to my productivity is that, for better or worse, I don't indulge much in either: hobbies or travel.

I don't enjoy travel and would much rather be home.

As for hobbies, parenting a special needs child and working the schedule I do leave little time for anything else.

What I really love to do is write. So work is my "hobby."

I like to read, and I have a few minor interests (e.g., a 92-gallon aquarium).

But I have no real major hobbies like collecting antiques or oil painting.

I do have a big comic book collection dating back to the early 1960s, but my sons have taken it over.

And I recently took a writing course here locally at The Writing Center in Englewood, NJ.

A boring life?

Maybe to you.

But it suits me just fine, thanks.

42

How I Got Where I am Today

"Bob, we want to know: how did you get involved in the business of copywriting, consulting, and information marketing?"

AM then goes on to ask a series of questions, assuring me that my readers want to know this stuff.

I sure hope he's right, because here are AM's questions about how I got into copywriting–and other private stuff–and my answers:

Q: Bob, what did you study in high school and college? What were your favorite subjects?

A: They were–and still are–science; especially chemistry, physics, and biology.

Q: How did you get into copywriting, Bob?

A: I majored in chemical engineering in college and have a B.S. from the University of Rochester.

When corporate recruiters interviewed me on campus, they discovered my strong interest in writing (I was on the college newspaper and magazine). A couple offered me positions as a staff writer, and I took one.

My first job out of college was as a junior marketing communications writer with Westinghouse. This was in 1979, and my salary was $18,500.

After only 18 months, a manufacturer of process equipment offered me a position as advertising manager for a lot more money–$27,000–and I took it. (While I have never been driven primarily by money, I had student loans to pay back.)

Q: How did that lead to freelancing?

A: Corporate life was not for me. I did too many things–going to endless meetings and managing our trade shows are two that come immediately to mind–that I had no interest in.

So I asked myself, "What part of my job do I like best, and can I do it freelance?" The answer was copywriting, and as I discovered, I could.

Q: What else didn't you like about corporate life? Bad bosses? Low pay? Office politics? Commuting?

A: I had great bosses, one of whom I am still good friends with today, more than 3 decades later.

I now earn more than 30 times the salary I made in my first corporate job, but I had no complaints about my pay back then...as I said, I've never been money oriented.

Office politics at both places were at a low to medium-low level, so they were tolerable.

I hate commuting, but always lived close to work. So my commutes were minimal.

Q: At what age did you start to work?

A: I got my first full-time adult job, at Westinghouse, upon graduating from the University of Rochester in 1979 at age 21.

I had a summer job every summer vacation. I also worked part-time as a dishwasher in the cafeteria throughout college.

My first summer job was clean-up and counter service at a swim club snack stand. I was 12 years old, and I earned $1.25 an hour.

Q: Where did you grow up? Have you lived in other places? Are you well-travelled?

A: I was born and went to elementary school in Paterson, NJ.

I have lived in New Jersey most of my life, outside of a year in Maryland while working at Westinghouse and a few years in Manhattan, on East 81st Street.

I am not well-travelled, although I have travelled on business (mainly to give seminars) to Germany, Poland, South Korea, England, Canada, France, Italy, and a few other places.

In point of fact, I dislike travel. I don't like airplanes (it's not fear–I just find the whole flying experience unpleasant). I don't like hotels, preferring to sleep in my own bed.

The bottom line is I'd rather be home. If that makes me shallow or unadventurous, so be it.

Q: Are you a vegetarian? Do you smoke or drink?

A: I do eat red meat if it is served to me, but I rarely cook or order it: I prefer vegetables, pasta, rice, beans, fruit, chicken, and fish. The exception is burgers, which I tend to order if we go to a chain restaurant like Applebees.

I love chopped liver, and since Dr. Al Sears says we need to eat organ meat, I treat myself to it every once in a while.

I do not smoke, and I only have a couple of beers on the weekends, my favorites being Guinness Stout and Taddy Porter.

Q: What are the most important things in your life?

A: First is family: my kids, wife, sister, and mother. Then helping other people improve their lives or their businesses through my writing.

Q: What are your hobbies?

A: I work 12 hours a day, so after that and spending time with my family, I don't have a lot of time or energy to invest in other interests.

I do think I should have a hobby, but nothing that I can realistically do calls strongly to me. I like to read, and I do have some other interests: music, nature, and learning new things.

I have a big 92-gallon aquarium and a large comic book collection. If I could be any comic book superhero, it would be the Flash–perhaps because I am a slow runner.

I played baritone saxophone and clarinet in high school and am toying with the idea of taking it up again.

Q: What is your favorite book?

A: Arthur Miller's "Death of a Salesman." The runner-up is probably John Irving's "A Prayer for Own Meany."

When I read for pure relaxation or escapism, Stephen King and Robert B. Parker are two of my favorites. King has been up and down in recent years, but I recently read "Duma Key" and loved it. Parker can be uneven but never fails to entertain.

I read a lot of science fiction as a kid and still do today. Favorite SF authors include Isaac Asimov, Harlan Ellison, Robert Silverberg, and Roger Zelazny. A book of my science fiction stories, "The Emancipation of Abraham Lincoln XL-3000 and Other Stories," is available on amazon.com.

Q: Do you watch TV?

A: I actually like TV as a medium, but can't find any shows these days that hold my attention. Of the shows I do occasionally watch, most are cartoons: The Simpsons, Family Guy, and once in a while South Park.

Q: Do you like movies?

A: Yes, but we don't go that often, so I see them mostly on cable. My recent favorites were Gran Torino, The Wrestler, Wolverine, and the new Star Trek based on the classic Wrath of Khan episode.

43

Why Some People Are Successful and Others Not

Why are some people more successful than others?

A lot of people who claim to be rich and successful—and I say "claim" because we don't know for a fact that they are—act as if it's all them...and that luck had nothing to do with it.

But the fact is, there are 6 specific factors that contribute to anyone's success or lack thereof—and luck is clearly one of them:

#1—Intelligence.

Some people are just smarter than others.

Intelligence is a result of genetics and environment—your upbringing.

Since heredity and the home you are born into are purely by chance, intelligence is largely a matter of luck.

By the way, by "smart" I don't mean "book smart."

I mean smart at anything that can make money—whether it's business, art, computers, or whatever.

#2—Knowledge.

Successful people are students for life.

They are constantly acquiring specific knowledge in their business or field—as well as a large storehouse of knowledge on all sorts of other topics.

As a rule, the more you learn, the more you earn.

#3–Effort.

The cliché about working smarter, not harder, is B.S.

Successful people work both smarter–and harder–than others.

#4–Attitude.

Successful people have an attitude. But it's not an attitude of ripping people off...or making as much money as they can any way they can.

It's an attitude of service: of giving their customers (and others) more value than they have any right to expect.

Many successful people are also goal-oriented, and it is important to them to become successful. So they focus their efforts on achievement of that goal.

#5–Aptitude.

We tend to be good at things we like and have an aptitude for.

Financially successful people just happen to have an aptitude and talent for things that make money.

Warren Buffett has said that the reason for his great wealth is that he was born with aptitudes and talents for which our society offers huge financial rewards.

Some of us are good at stuff, but not stuff that pays well. And if we pursue those interests exclusively, our incomes can be limited as a result.

#6–Luck.

As you can see, the key success factors of intelligence (#1) and aptitudes (#5) are determined mainly by chance–and are largely beyond our control.

Yes, Warren Buffett studied finance, worked hard, and had the right attitude.

But he was also lucky, as is virtually every person who has achieved significant wealth, success, or accomplishment in life.

The honest ones admit this and are thankful.

Any rich or successful person who said luck had no part in his achievement is either in denial or unwilling to come clean.

Therefore, if you are successful, you should be humble, not arrogant and boastful.

After all, you were lucky. Right?

44

How to Find Your Niche in Life

How do you find a niche that fits you?

Perform a simple self-audit.

Here are the 10 questions you should ask yourself when picking your niche.

As you think of the answers, write them down:

>>What do I like?

>>What am I interested in?

>>What am I good at?

>>What do I have an aptitude for?

>>What is my education?

>>What do I know?

>>What is my experience?

>>What have I accomplished?

>>Which of the above areas has the least competition?

>> Which of the above areas pays high rates?

For the above categories, list as many items under each category as you possibly can on index cards, one per card.

Once you have completed your lists, look them over, and set aside the cards for any items that look like possible niches.

Next, pick the five most interesting potential niches. Put the cards in order of preference.

Now look at the list. Chances are that one or two of these subjects are things people routinely pay to learn about.

Pick one and you've found your niche. As Aristotle said, "Where your passions intersect with the needs of the public, therein lies your vocation."

What if none of the five items on your list is appealing to you as a niche? Pick the next best five items from your index cards and repeat the process until you have a niche you are enthusiastic about.

45

Useful Rules of Thumb for Internet Marketers

Here are a few convenient rules of thumb to keep in mind as you start up and operate your own Internet marketing business:

1–The 10/10 rule.

This rule says always give your online customers a discount off the list price, but the discount doesn't have to be huge; either 10% or $10 off will do.

2–The 99/1 rule.

99% of your affiliate sales will come from 1% of your affiliates.

3–The 90/90 rule.

90% of the people who opt into your e-list who are going to buy something from you do so within 90 days.

Therefore you want to get as many new subscribers as possible to make a purchase within that time frame–otherwise, they may never buy.

4–The 3-month ROI rule.

This rule applies to buying traffic and new names for your e-list.

It says that ideally the revenue generated by new names added to your list should pay back the advertising cost to acquire those new names within 3 months. If not, you may be paying too much per name.

5–The 10 X 10 = 100 rule.

If you can increase your click through rates and conversion rates each tenfold, you will increase your revenues one hundredfold.

6–The 8:1 rule.

The minimum selling price of a product should be at least 8 times the cost of the goods. So a DVD set that costs $10 to make must sell for at least $80.

7–The 0.1% rule.

Each time you broadcast an e-mail to your list, no more than 0.1% of your subscribers should unsubscribe.

For a list of 100,000 subscribers, that would be a maximum of 100 opting out of the list.

If your opt-out rate exceeds 0.1%, consider throttling back on frequency or improving the content.

46

The 25-50-25 Rule of Time Management

There are only three ways to learn either a new process (e.g., starting an Internet business) or a new skill (e.g., copywriting): studying, observing, and doing.

The 25-50-25 rule says that to master a skill or process, and put what you learn into practical action, you must divide your time as follows:

>> No more than 25% of your time is spent studying–i.e., reading books, going to boot camps, attending workshops, dialing into tele-seminars, listening to CDs in your car.

>> No more than 25% of your time is spent observing–watching what successful people in your field are already doing; e.g., if you want to become a direct mail copywriter, this means reading and analyzing the direct mail you get in your mailbox each day.

>> At least 50% of your time is spent actually DOING the thing you are studying and observing–e.g., if you want to sell information products on the Internet, you are creating your first product...designing your Website...or building your list.

Acquiring business knowledge is a worthwhile activity. But without action, that knowledge is worthless to you.

Here's a little secret that may be helpful: You don't have to know everything—or even most of what there is to know—to succeed in most endeavors.

For example, there are hundreds of strategies for making money on the Internet.

But you can make a six-figure annual income online using only a few of them, even if you never bother to learn the others.

When we were kids, our parents and teachers told us to study, study, study.

But I see many people today much more enamored with studying and reading about business, marketing, freelancing, and entrepreneurship than actually doing.

Well, I understand that. Reading about marketing is fascinating—and fun. And it's within your comfort zone.

But the money is in the doing, not the reading.

Follow the 25-50-25 rule, and you'll be doing—and making money—at least half the time.

47

Paying More Than the Sticker Price

When it comes to Internet marketing, there is a whole slew of vendors who work incredibly cheaply.

For instance, one gal, a fitness expert, offered to write a 500-word article for $30.

If I hired her, I would not pay her $30. I would pay her anywhere from $100 to $200.

Here's the main reason: When you find people desperate enough to work for peanuts...

Or you squeeze a vendor and get him to lower his price to the bare minimum...

Those people don't feel good about working for you, because they are not making a fair wage.

As a result, most of these underpaid freelancers resent their clients.

They also try to complete the job as fast as they can, so they will make a little more per hour.

Result: they rush their work, not putting much care in it. And this shows in the inferior finished product.

Once, as an experiment, I hired a cheap writer from elance to write an article on careers in chemistry for my chemistry web site www.mychemset.com.

His first sentence – and I kid you not – was: "Chemistry is a good career for people who are fond of atoms."

Lots of graphic designers, writers, voice over artists, and other serving the Internet marketing industry charge prices so low, they are earning less than minimum wage.

No one should be paid less than minimum wage, and I will never pay any freelance that little.

Yes, there are all sorts of service professionals and vendors you can talk down in price if you play hard ball, because many are hungry and need the work.

But don't do it. Pay a fair wage, and you'll get a happier vendor who does a better job for you.

"What difference does it make
what it *is*? You get one *free*!"

48

The Secret of the Takeaway Close

A few years ago I came across a brochure for an independent consultant, Sommers White.

The brochure promoting White's consulting services was written entirely in question and answer format. But what really caught my eye was the first Q & A in the lead:

Q: Why should I hire Sommers White?

A: Perhaps you should not.

Why is this opening so effective?

First, it is unexpected. The surprise factor gets your attention.

Second, it instantly builds White's credibility. Obviously, here is a guy who only wants clients he can help. He won't just take any business. He has to believe he can really help you before he will work with you. What an ethical guy!

Third, it actually enhances the desire to find out more about White and possibly hire him. It's intriguing. Who is this man of mystery? Why is he so sure of himself that he doesn't even want your business?

This technique of selling is called "the takeaway close." White did not invent it, although his use of it as a lead is unusual.

The basic premise of the takeaway close is: People want what they can't have.

Think about it. Your doctor tells you, "No more candy." What do you instantly want? Candy!

Sales trainer Paul Karasik recommends you use the takeaway method when trying to close a sale with a reluctant prospect.

If the prospect is hemming and hawing, shut your notebook or folder, take the contract off the table, and say, "You know, you're right. This may not be for you."

The prospect will immediately want to know why you say this, and often, will try to prove you wrong. In essence, they'll start selling YOU on changing your mind and accepting them as a customer. What an ideal situation for you!

Another thing that makes the takeaway close so effective is what I call the power of the contrary: When you do something people don't expect, it is an instant attention-getter.

A radio commercial for Seaman's, a furniture store in my area, begins: "Whatever you do, DON'T buy furniture today!"

You don't expect a furniture store to tell you not to buy furniture. So you listen. It sounds like you are going to get helpful consumer advice—maybe tips on shopping for furniture.

Turns out, the tip is to wait until Saturday for Seaman's big blowout sale. But it works. They got your attention—and now you want to wait for their sale.

The next time you are having trouble closing a prospect or moving a sale forward, try the takeaway close.

One caveat: You have to be willing to lose the sale to make this work. You must be prepared for and ready to accept the possibility that the prospect will say, "Yes, you're right, this is not for me."

Therefore, the takeaway close should only be used either: (a) when you already have more business than you can handle—and therefore can afford to lose the sale, or (b) when the sale is stalled and you cannot move the prospect forward using your other closing techniques.

49

Overcoming Price Resistance

In the movie Tin Men starring Richard Dreyfus and Danny DeVito, an aluminum siding salesman goes into a car dealership to buy a new Cadillac.

"How much is it?" he asks the car salesman about the car he wants to buy.

"How much do you want to pay?" the car salesman asks back.

Disgusted by what is an obvious sales tactic, he replies sarcastically, "A dollar...I want to pay a dollar."

Many of us won't ask the prospect how much he or she wants to pay because we feel that it is somehow sleazy, and that doing so will create an uncomfortable situation.

But if you indeed did know how much your buyers wanted to spend, your sales closing ratio would shoot through the roof—because you'd be quoting prices you knew they could afford and were willing and prepared to spend.

How do you ascertain what the buyer wants to spend without the awkwardness of asking outright?

When it's time to discuss price, ask the buyer, "Do you have a budget?"

Note that you are not asking "What is your budget?" You are instead asking the much less threatening question, "Do you have a budget?"

The buyer can only give one of two answers: yes or no, with about half of prospects saying yes and the other half saying no.

If the buyer says "yes," then you ask: "Would you mind sharing with me what your budget is?"

Those prospects who tell you their budget have just given you the range under which your price quotation must fall to be accepted.

But what if the buyer says, "No, we don't have a budget." Then you ask: "Well, do you have a dollar figure in mind of what you would like it to cost?"

Even if they do not have a budget worked out, many people, when asked the question in this way, will come back at you with an answer something like "I was figuring to spend around $1,000 and not more than $3,000."

In effect, they really do have a budget—$1,000 to $3,000—but just never wrote it down or said it out loud before.

A few people, however, will not share their budget no matter how you ask. "I don't want to give you my budget," they will say. "I want you to tell me what it will cost."

In such cases, use the "good, better, best" method of price quotation.

Let's say you are quoting on selling the prospect a half-acre lot with a custom built home.

Instead of just quoting your top-end home, which is $500,000, you give the prospect three options to choose from.

The first option, which you call "good," is a basic three-bedroom home with a fireplace and unfinished basement. It is $300,000—the cheapest you can offer while still giving the buyer a decent home and yourself a decent profit.

The second option, which you call "better," is the same home, but with a finished basement and an added sitting room in the master bedroom suite. It is $400,000—your middle-of-the-road model.

The third option, which you call "best," is the same home as in the "better" option but with top-of-the-line landscaping, a second fireplace, and a fourth bedroom. It is $500,000—your top-of-the-line model.

You outline all options for the prospect, including the prices. Then instead of asking him whether he wants a home, you ask him, "Which do you want—good, better, or best?"

This strategy increases the chances that your price quotation will fall within the dollar amount the prospect wants to pay.

Also, very few people want the lowest-quality of three choices. So some buyers who were looking to pay $300,000 will find a way to pay $400,000 (even if it means a bigger mortgage or borrowing from Uncle Joe)—and more will select "better" over "good."

50

Internet Marketing's Dirty Little Secret

The worst niche to get into if you want to become an Internet marketer is to sell info products on Internet marketing.

It's a terrible niche for you – for 2 reasons.

First, it's grossly overcrowded. Because Internet marketing IS such a good business, lots of people have jumped on teaching it to others.

Second, if you're a newbie, then you really don't know enough about Internet marketing to teach it.

You are competing against guys like Rich Scheffren, Joe Vitale, Terry Dean, and Perry Marshall who know about a zillion times more about Internet marketing than you do.

Another situation to avoid is to teach Internet marketing when the only thing you have ever done is teach Internet marketing.

The real-world marketing experience of many Internet marketers is severely limited.

Aside from courses on Internet marketing, they have sold no other products.

That's not true of the top players, though.

Rich Scheffren had a successful retail business.

Perry Marshall sold industrial products.

Joe Vitale wrote copy selling a wide range of products.

I have written copy selling everything from vitamins and stock market newsletters, to chemicals and golf products, to industrial equipment and $30 million corporate jets.

To be a genuine marketing expert, you MUST move beyond just selling information on marketing and gain experience in marketing other products, both info products as well as merchandise.

And don't pick Internet marketing as your topic niche for your online business.

Pick your hobby ... or something that really interests you ... or something you do at your 9 to 5 jobs ... or a business skill you can teach.

One fellow I know built a successful online business around dogs.

Another created info products teaching Excel applications.

I started with marketing as my niche because that's been my whole life so it made sense for me.

But if I were starting over today, I wouldn't touch the marketing niche with a 10-foot pole.

51

Do You Treat Customers Right?

At a recent meeting of the Ethical Culture Society of Bergen County—a group whose members are like-minded humanists—a speaker said that a precept of the organization is:

"Every person deserves to be treated fairly and kindly."

This is great advice especially if you are an Internet marketer. Because from what I see, there are many Internet marketers who don't follow this rule.

I hear complaints all the time from people. They tell me they bought a product online, but when they called about returning it, the Internet marketer became abrupt and rude.

Or they tell me about Internet marketers who flat out refuse, on the flimsiest of excuses, to honor their money-back guarantees.

I hear horror stories of Internet marketers who recruit affiliates, let them generate sales, and then don't send commission checks.

A lot of consumers are frustrated that Internet marketers are so darn inaccessible.

I mean, if you have a problem with your phone line, you can call the phone company and eventually get a real person on the phone, right?

But when you want to complain to an Internet marketer, there more often than not is no mailing address or phone number.

And when you send them an e-mail, you get a response from a robot–an auto-responder–and not a live human being.

The e-mail tells you how busy the marketer is. Sometimes it promises a return call from a person...which usually never comes.

The collective sigh of all the Internet customers who despair at the treatment they receive from Internet marketers is palpable.

"But," you argue, "I can't personally respond to each complaint. That's what I have an auto-responder or an assistant for."

First of all, assuming your products are a good value, you're not getting all that many complaints to begin with.

Second of all, you probably could respond to all of them, if you wanted to.

SL, a major catalog marketer, writes a personal note of apology–and sends it along with a small gift– whenever his rather large catalog company gets an unhappy customer.

If SL can do it, you and I can do it too.

But let's say you are busy, and can personally respond to only a fraction of the complaints you get. What should you do?

Well, I hired a part-time assistant in my Internet marketing business, and it's her job to handle all complaints and special requests, which she does with sensitivity and common sense.

However, I see all the complaints first, and I pick certain ones to handle personally.

If you do the same, which customers should you give extra special attention to?

There are two types: (1) the excellent customer and (2) the extremely unhappy customer.

The excellent customer is someone who can't stop buying your products, has been easy to service, and raves about you to everyone he knows.

Only now they are asking for something a bit out of the ordinary—and have created a special situation that must be handled.

Since satisfied customers are your most important asset, you want to go to extremes to keep these extremely happy customers happy.

For instance, one wanted to substitute for the free bonus report I was offering one of my e-books—something we don't give away.

But he had bought tons from us, so I happily gave it to him.

The other type of customer you want to handle personally and with great care is the extremely unhappy customer.

Reason: unhappy customers tell other people. The more unhappy they become, the more people they complain about you to—and the louder they say it.

In the good old days, an unhappy customer told maybe 5 or 10 other people.

But with social networking, they can tell thousands with a few key strokes and mouse clicks.

I had a problem with a product I bought online, but could get no satisfaction from the seller, who refused to even take my call.

So I wrote about it on my blog.

Within 24 hours, the marketer called, apologized profusely, immediately fixed the problem, and begged me to remove the post from my blog.

I have heard of Internet marketers who blow their stacks at customers, particularly older customers, who aren't that computer literate and have trouble opening and reading an e-book or downloading and listening to a podcast.

They may frustrate you and try your patience, but think about how frustrated they must feel. They just bought great content from you, and now they can't access it.

Every person deserves to be treated fairly and kindly. Are you treating every customer and prospect fairly? Do you do it angrily or kindly?

One more thing: add unadvertised grace periods to your money-back guarantees.

For instance, if you have a 90-day money-back guarantee and the customer returns your product on day 92, should you give him his money back anyway?

Yes, because you want to treat him fairly and kindly...just like you'd want to be treated when returning an item to a store.

And if you treat your customers fairly and kindly, they will deal with you in the same way.

52

Is Marketing Necessary?

One of my copywriting assignments is to write an occasional e-mail promotion for the American Writers and Artists Institute.

These e-mail messages often go out with my name in the "From" line–and recently Jim, a recipient, didn't take too kindly to my telling him about a new AWAI product via the e-mail marketing medium.

And he told me so in a rather rude (and I think uncalled for) e-mail message sent to me personally.

When I called him to task for his rudeness, he apologized, but then added this statement:

"What is really sad today, since the birth of the Internet, is that any marketer can send 1 million e-mails out to people that really never asked for them."

I can understand that. Some people don't like getting telemarketing calls (I'm one of them). Some people don't like direct mail. Some people hate TV commercials.

My father-in-law, for example, installs a special clicker on every new TV he buys. Whenever a commercial comes on, he clicks it. The picture is still displayed, but the sound is cut off. When the show is back on, he clicks it again to restore the audio.

So fine. But Jim wasn't done with me. He then added a comment that can only be taken as a put-down:

"And for you to have to market your wares, by dunning, via e-mail, shows that what you have is not in really big demand anyway."

Of course, addicted as I am to educating people about the realities of the free market system we live in, I immediately sent Jim the following reply:

"Thanks for your gracious note. But...

"You are as wrong as wrong can be when you say: 'And for you to have to market your wares, by dunning, via e-mail, shows that what you have is not in really big demand anyway.'

"The objective of any business entity is to make a profit for its owners or shareholders while servicing its customers.

"Marketing online (or any other way) achieves both objectives...

"First, the marketing generates increased sales of the product. If the sales exceed the cost of the marketing, it is profitable.

"That is why email marketing works—the cost is low, so it's easier to break even vs. TV commercials which are more expensive to produce.

"Second, the more people you can sell your product to, the more that can benefit from it.

"I have the feeling that you think marketing or selling is unethical, sleazy, or demeaning.

"If you are selling a product or service you truly believe in, it is the opposite, bringing the benefits of that product or service to the masses so that many more people can be helped by it.

"If I buy into your argument, then anyone who sends out resumes when looking for a new job is not a competent employee, because if he were, he would be in demand at all times and besieged by constant job offers.

"As for me not being 'in demand,' I have more clients and assignments than I could ever possibly hope to handle and turn down dozens every year who want to hire me.

"You can also read articles explaining e-mail marketing for free on the articles page of my Website www.bly.com."

Why am I including this rant here? Because it teaches a simple lesson that is extremely important to your marketing success.

If you are caught up in the mistaken belief that marketing, selling, and advertising are somehow sleazy...

Or if you inherently believe money and profit are evil...

Then you are not going to market or sell yourself, your company, or your product or service enthusiastically–and your lack of enthusiasm will impact upon your results.

The only kind of marketing that I find distasteful or distressful is to sell a product or service you don't really believe in, don't really like, and don't think is any good.

In such cases, you are merely trying to take people's money without exchanging something of value for it—so naturally, you feel guilty, and the whole transaction seems tainted.

But if you offer a quality product or service, priced fairly—and backed by a strong guarantee which you honor—then you should feel proud, not guilty.

In fact, you'd be doing people a disservice by NOT marketing your product actively and aggressively...

Because then they'd never know about it or have the opportunity to benefit from what you offer.

Right?

53

Why My E-Mails are Not Spam

Last week, I told how a recipient of an e-mail marketing message I had written for a client lambasted and insulted me for sending it.

When I took him to task for it in this column, reader Kevin R. jumped to the man's defense.

"It seems as though you are missing a crucial distinction that sets apart e-mail communications from more traditional forms of advertising," wrote Kevin. "This distinction can best be summarized as a property rights issue.

"When one is watching television or reading a magazine, there is no surprise in encountering an advertisement there. By watching a television channel, purchasing a magazine, or even driving by a billboard, the consumer has 'purchased' (although the cost may be zero) another person's property. The content placed into that medium is solely determined by the producer, and they have every right to include advertising if they choose.

"E-mail is not the same. An e-mail inbox is the property of the owner, just as a real-world mailbox belongs to the homeowner. An advertiser who sends unsolicited e-mail is trespassing upon that property without the consent of the owner.

"It is the same situation as if you broke into someone's house and left flyers on their dining room table, or erected a billboard on their property in the middle of the night. E-mail may be cheap, but nothing in this world is free. Unsolicited e-mail consumes the bandwidth, storage space, and attention of the recipient without their consent.

"I receive many advertisements that I immediately throw away unread. I do not complain about these because they come from sources, like Agora, that I have voluntarily signed up for. E-mail from unknown, unwanted sources, however, receives my full scorn and wrath. I will not purchase any product that is advertised in this fashion, no matter how appealing it looks.

"I hope this gives you a different perspective on the issue of unsolicited e-mails, and causes you to rethink whether they are a good form of advertising."

Sorry, Kevin, but I think you have missed the boat here. Let me tell you why I believe your argument is wrong.

Legal e-mail marketing is only sent to "opt in" lists where the people on the list have agreed to receive such messages when they registered on a Website, signed up for a free e-zine, or whatever.

Therefore they gave up the rights Kevin is talking about when they subscribed or registered for the free content or whatever got them on the list in the first place.

If you don't want e-mail marketing, don't register or subscribe if the marketer is asking you to agree to receive "e-mails on offers of interest."

When I mentioned all this to Kevin, he heartily agreed: "In your case, Bob, had the complaining person signed up for the content that he received? If so, then he had no reason to complain."

Where the problem comes in, I think, is that people are unaware that they have opted in and agreed to receive promotional e-mails in exchange for getting a free e-zine or Web content.

Yes, the registration form for the Website they accessed or the sign-up box for the free e-zine they subscribed to may have mentioned that they were agreeing to receive e-mail messages—not only from the Website owner or e-zine publisher but also from marketers offering related products and services.

But most of us don't really pay attention to this "fine print." So the recipient who blasts you for sending him an unsolicited e-mail probably doesn't remember that he "opted in" and agreed to receive it, even when you remind him of this fact.

One solution is to remind the recipient, in the lead of your e-mail message, that he requested it or at least agreed to view it.

Here's the reminder I place at the top of every issue of my free monthly e-zine, which you can subscribe to by visiting www.bly.com:

"You are getting this e-mail because you subscribed to it on www.bly.com or because you are one of Bob's clients, prospects, seminar attendees, or book buyers. If you would prefer not to receive further e-mails of this type, go to www.bly.com, enter your e-mail address, and hit Unsubscribe."

For a solo e-mail marketing message, I recommend including language along these lines:

"We respect your online time and privacy, and pledge not to abuse this medium. If you prefer not to receive further e-mails from us of this type, please reply to this e-mail and type 'Remove' in the subject line."

As for whether e-mails are a "good form of marketing," it boils down to this: Can you make money with e-mail marketing?

My clients and I are generating millions of dollars in sales of products and services using e-mail marketing—sales that, in the past, would have to be generated using more expensive, traditional marketing vehicles, such as direct mail.

54

Not Every Opinion Has Value

The other day I got the following unsolicited e-mail from a Web designer trying to get me to hire him to redesign my Website:

"I just visited your site to check your copywriting service.

"You have a very good portfolio, but one thing that your Website lacks is powerful design that would reflect such quality service.

"It is just happened that I offer redesign service, so I decided to email you.

"I have a lot of top-quality design templates to choose from. I also provide full customization/optimization service.

"You have a truly professional service and background, so I believe your online 'look & feel' should not be worse. If you are interested let me know.

"Sincerely, Paul V., Web Site Designer."

Can you spot all the mistakes in Paul's e-mail to me?

1. It is an unsolicited promotional e-mail sent to an e-mail address where the recipient has not "opted in"– that is, has not agreed to receive such messages. Therefore, it is spam. Not a great way to start a relationship.

2. The first sentence is misleading. He makes himself sound like a prospect interested in my copywriting services...which he is not.

3. In the second paragraph, Paul gives me a critique of my Website–a critique I did not ask for and therefore place no value upon (especially since I have never heard of Paul).

4. Also, Paul's critique is negative. So he is insulting me within the first two sentences of our conversation–and I don't even know who he is...continuing to start us off on the wrong foot.

5. In the ungrammatical sentence in the third paragraph, he shows his true colors. He is not giving an objective critique with any real value. He is simply trying to peddle his services–without knowing a single thing about me, my goals, or my level of satisfaction (or dissatisfaction) with my current Website.

6. The phrase "it is just happened" has all the sincerity of a three-dollar bill. It's obvious that this guy spends his time writing to Website owners in the desperate hope that they'll give him some money.

7. The fifth paragraph again insults the recipient, telling him that his Website is "worse" and should not be.

It's a common ploy that many service marketers–usually those without much business and desperate for some revenue–think will work: Tell someone their Widget (or whatever) sucks, and that you can make it better...if only they would hire you.

It seldom works. Here's why...

To begin with, you're offering unsolicited advice...which, trust me, is absolutely the worst kind (I intend to write a whole column on the pitfalls of unsolicited advice, so prevalent has it become in the Internet age).

The work you are criticizing may very well have been done by the person to whom you are aiming the criticism...so you are insulting a complete stranger. An odd way to get people to like you (and remember, people usually do business only with people they like or trust).

Also, you are giving a subjective opinion for which you don't have the facts to back it up.

In the example above, Paul has no idea of how well my Website is working, whether it is achieving its sales goals, or even what those objectives are.

So how is he in a position to judge whether what he sees is working?

He's not, which reduces his already marginal credibility with me to virtually zero.

So, what's the root of the problem?

It's this: To be a successful marketer, you've got to solve a problem that's important to the customer.

To solve a problem that's important to the customer, you've first got to identify what problems the client has, and then identify those that are most important and urgent.

When you give unsolicited advice or criticism like Paul did with my Website, you have NO IDEA what the other person's problems, needs, or priorities are.

You are giving advice in a vacuum—the total opposite of what a competent professional would do.

What's a better approach Paul could have taken with me?

One might be to ask, "If there's one thing you would want to change or improve about your Website, what would it be?"

Or he could have offered to share with me some new Web marketing techniques that he has used for his other clients—techniques that worked well for them and that I might be interested in knowing about.

Or any of a dozen approaches other than to pretend to give me an objective critique when in reality he is delivering a blatant sales pitch.

55

Nobody Gets Away

On a routine visit to the doctor, he said my legs were slightly swollen because fluid was collecting in them.

He prescribed that I get a support pillow and sleep with my legs elevated at night. He also told me to stay away from the salt shaker. If that doesn't work, I would have to wear compression socks.

This may seem a small thing, but it was a bit traumatic, because it reminds me of my father.

He had terrible varicose veins, slept with a wedge pillow to elevate his legs, and wore compression stocks.

So in my mind, my having to do the same makes me feel like I am getting old – which is perhaps appropriate, because I am getting older. We all are.

My solution that day was to go to the gym and work out like a maniac to convince myself I am not yet ready for the old folks' home.

But no matter how hard we try, we are all at some point have an increasing number of ills small and large – no matter how healthy a lifestyle we live.

For instance, you can run marathons, bench 350, eat right, load up on supplements – and still get cancer.

Sure, you can take steps to stay healthy and fit much longer than the average Joe, but no one escapes aging and death. No one.

That's why I laugh when some millennial Internet marketing whippersnapper mocks me for being 58. What he does not realize is that HE will be 58 in the blink of an eye. I wonder if he will find it so contemptible then.

The sad fact is that everyone on the planet is dying, and in a little over a hundred years, everyone alive today will likely be dead.

My way of making this dark fate palatable has always been to do work I love and dedicate myself to my business.

The great David Ogilvy was fond of quoting this Scottish proverb: "Be happy while you're living, for you're a long time dead."

"Where's the support group for people who are **addicted** to support groups?"

The Lobster family reunion goes terribly wrong.

56

Why Your Marketing Doesn't Work

Some time ago, I listened to a talk given by Joseph Sugarman, founder of JS&A and widely recognized as one of the greatest mail order marketers of all time.

JS&A is the company that sells those Blue Blocker sunglasses you see advertised on TV and in magazines.

The glasses really work, by the way. Put a pair on, and everything blue is converted to a shade of gray.

Anyway, during the talk, Mr. Sugarman mentioned that he often tested three or four different ads for the same product...and in some cases as many as 10 different versions!

"Typically, nine of the ads would fail but one would work spectacularly well," said Mr. Sugarman, "The profits from that one ad would more than cover the losses from the other nine."

Do you do that...create multiple ads and then test them to see which works best?

Or do you—like most small businesses—create and test just one ad...or one postcard ...or one e-mail...or one sales letter or direct mail package?

If so, you are significantly reducing your odds of getting a winning promotion...

The reason is that not all promotions work. In fact, most don't.

Say one out of four promotions is a winner. And that's being optimistic.

Jerry Huntsinger, a well-known copywriter in fundraising, once told me "9 out of 10 of the things I do don't work."

And in his speech, Joseph Sugarman reported similar results...sometimes having to write and test 10 ads to get one winner.

But let's stick with the "one winner out of every four tests" figure for now.

Based on those odds, if you run just one ad, or mail just one version of a sales letter, your chances of hitting a winner are only one out of four...and the odds are 75% that your marketing effort will bomb.

What commonly happens is that a small business decides to "try" direct mail...send out a poorly written, amateurish letter or postcard...and when they get no responses, proclaim that "direct mail doesn't work."

Sure it doesn't...tell that to Nightingale-Conant...or Boardroom...or Publishers Clearinghouse...or Day Timer.

On the other hand, if you create and test four different ads or letter versions, the odds are in your favor that at least one will work and be profitable for you.

My rule of thumb for improving direct marketing results is: Look at what the big players—the successful direct marketers—are doing. And do what they do.

And the one thing every successful direct marketer has in common is...they test. A lot.

What do they test?

Headlines... outer envelopes... direct mail formats... copy approaches... sales appeals... mailing lists... prices... offers... guarantees... terms... anything with the potential to generate a big lift in response rates. Or even a small one, for that matter.

Does all this testing make sense?

On one such test, a marketer increased response to an e-mail marketing message by 50%... just by changing the subject line.

In another test, a software company increased orders from a direct mail package tenfold...simply by varying the wording of the offer.

And a computer school doubled the response rate to its newspaper advertising when they added the offer of a free career booklet.

Does all this testing make sense?

You bet it does!

Imagine...just by changing a few words on a piece of paper or a computer screen, you can double your sales...revenues...and profits.

If there's another area of business that gives you that kind of leverage, I'd like to hear about it.

One other point...

In direct marketing, no one can predict with any degree of certainty which ad or mailing is going to work.

You only learn what works by testing and keeping track of the results.

You may have your subjective opinions about what you like and don't like in advertising...we all do...

But in direct marketing, you simply can't argue with results.

57

It's Not a Bad Life

One of the supposed advantages of freelancing is getting to do what you want to do.

But I never have that.

I spend my life doing what other people want to do – specifically, my family.

For instance, my wife wants to spend a tidy sum redoing two of our bathrooms which, to me, look perfectly fine.

What's the upshot? The contractor has been hired and the deposit paid. Never mind what I want.

Earlier this year my wife and older son wanted to take a trip to England, but (a) I was really too busy to go and (b) I hate travel and had no desire to go.

Before you know it, I found myself on a plane to London.

Last year, they decided they were tired of living in our town in Bergen county NJ and wanted to move to more bucolic Morris county.

I hate moving and think you are crazy to do it if you do not have to.

Well, guess what? Now we are living in a new home in Morris county.

After 32 years of marriage, I am used to not getting my way.

Does it bother me? Well, yes and no.

Yes in that I would rather not do things I do not want to do, or spend money buying things I do not want to own.

On the other hand, these things make my wife and kids happy. And their happiness is the most important thing in the world to me – much more so than my own.

They – not what I do or what I buy – are what I live for.

So I am happy to indulge them.

Although it would be nice to get my way once in a while.

58

A Simple Tip for People Who Work at Home

Recently, I came into the office in the morning and found a voice mail.

It was from a freelance copywriter asking me to call her.

Now, this is no surprise: I regularly get calls from novice copywriters asking for advice about the freelance copywriting business.

When I called her back, around 8am EST (I normally get to work 7am), she answered the phone in a hoarse, dazed voice...and I knew I had woken her up.

I immediately felt guilty...but I should not have.

After all, why is it MY responsibility to know or think about whether she works at home?

And what difference should that make to clients, prospects, or anyone else who calls her?

Sure enough, she told me, a bit grumpily, "It is 5am where I am."

And I felt vaguely scolded...as if I was supposed to figure out her location and time zone from the area code in the phone number she had left on my voice mail!

A major component of your small business marketing is the professional impression and image you convey...and that requires home-based businesses to have two separate phone lines: one for home, and one for business.

The rules are simple...

* Always answer the business phone promptly, clearly, and professionally. Pick it up on the second ring. The first seems too needy, and by the fourth, the prospect is getting annoyed by the long wait.

* Identity yourself and your company in your greeting, e.g., "Flowers by Fiona, this is Fiona speaking."

* The business phone should ONLY be answered by people from the business—never children, parents, or the cleaning lady.

* When the business phone rings after hours and you do not feel like talking to business callers, don't answer it. Let the voice mail pick it up.

* Keep the business phone in a private office or other area shielded from the sounds of home life. Business callers should not hear kids fighting or babies crying in the background.

* Do not require the caller to think about your situation, e.g., that they are calling late or reaching you at home.

That's not their concern or responsibility...and having to worry about that is a turn-off for your clients and prospects.

For instance, I once called AC, a freelance PR consultant at 5pm; I suspected he worked at home, but did not know that for certain.

When he answered, he sounded annoyed and didn't hide it well; clearly, I had done something wrong.

"Is there something wrong?" I asked.

"I am eating dinner," he replied testily.

Apparently, he required me to be a mind reader or have surveillance cameras in his house.

Or maybe he was living in the 1950s, when most people actually left work at 5pm on the dot!

Another faux pas that can damage the professional image you want to convey.

If someone calls and the person they want to reach is not available, take a message and promise to have that person call back promptly.

Do NOT, as some businesses do, amazingly to me, is say, "He's not here right now. Can you call back later?"

This adds another task to the prospect's to-do list for the day. And your job is to make the prospect's life easier, not add more work to it.

Finally, here's the "technology" set up I recommend for home-based business phone systems:

* Separate phone lines for home and business.

* Another separate, dedicated phone line for the fax machine. It's annoying and amateurish to tell prospects, "Let me hang up on you. I will unplug the phone, plug in the fax, and then you can call back and fax your document." It is disrespectful because it wastes the prospect's time.

* And yes, yet another dedicated phone line for the modem if you have a dial-up connection to the Internet.

However, I'd recommend high-speed broadband access, which is faster and does not require its own phone line.

The point: even if you work at home, you are in business and you are a business professional.

Therefore, you have to convey a professional image that says you are serious about business, not a dilettante playing around between jobs.

59

Don't be a Typo Nazi

When I tell you this story, you may think it makes me look like a jerk.

But it conveys an important lesson for every entrepreneur and marketing professional.

And the lesson is this: to communicate effectively, it's incumbent upon YOU to really understand the other person—what they think, what they want, what's important to them—and NOT the other way around.

Okay. So here's what happened...

A person I don't know called me at work out of the blue the other day—while I was frantically writing to meet a deadline.

"I am reading your book," he said, naming one of my books. "There is a typo on page 383," he said triumphantly, as if dropping the biggest bombshell since Hiroshima.

"Thanks, but you don't need to tell me about it," I said politely.

He stammered, absolutely stunned.

I knew it was not the response he was looking for.

From past calls like this, he expected me to write down the information he was about to give me, and possibly engage me in dialogue...which a lot of book readers want to do with authors.

Instead, I simply thanked him for calling, and ended the call.

I didn't lecture him on the realities of life, but if I had, here's what I would have said:

"Sir, I don't know you, and I am not sure why you feel compelled to take time out of your day, call me up, and report that there is a typo in one of my books–or what kind of satisfaction it gives you.

"But I've written almost 80 books, totaling more than 16,000 pages. I am sure there are a number of typos within those 16,000 pages.

"The book you are referring to I wrote more than 20 years ago. It's already printed, and is not going to be reprinted again. So there's nothing I can do about the typo you've found.

"Also, I have a dozen projects on my desk this week, all with deadlines. To finish this work and run my business, I have about a hundred tasks on my priority list.

"So taking a look at my printed books–and fixing typos in them–wouldn't even make the list. In fact, it's not even on my radar as far as 'important things to do' is concerned. Sorry to disappoint you, but that's the reality of life."

As I said at the beginning of this article: you may find my response to my anonymous proofreader offensive. After all, wasn't he just trying to do me a kindness?

In my experience, that's possible.

But from two and a half decades of getting such calls as an author, I have found that kindness is often not the primary motivation behind such calls.

Often the caller revels in showing the published writer that he made a mistake.

Or, he hopes that the author will become a friend or (unpaid) advisor—and that pointing out the typo will open up a relationship in some way.

But the point is this: if you want to communicate with someone effectively...and establish a relationship, whether personal or business...you have to, as the cliché points out, "put yourself in the customer's shoes"...whether you're selling a product, service, or idea.

As a marketer, it's imperative that you understand the CUSTOMER...what he thinks, wants, needs, fears, and desires...what's important to him—NOT what's important to you.

In the example of my anonymous proofreader, for example, a better way to establish the contact with me might have been as follows:

"Bob, this is Joe. I'm reading your book and I have one item in it I'd like to briefly discuss with you. It will take less than a minute. Do you have time now?"

This approach, by the way, works beautifully in selling—either when cold calling or following up on inquiries.

People are busy today, and they cannot abide it when others don't respect their time or understand just how pressured they are.

I ALWAYS ask when calling someone I don't know: "Is this a bad time for you?" If they say yes, I ask when would be a better time to talk.

He could have continued: "I found a typo in the book. Do you want to know about it?"

This is also a good strategy in selling: before launching into your "pitch," ask the prospect for permission to proceed.

If you want to communicate or establish a relationship with other people, it's your JOB to understand them and where they're coming from...and asking questions is one way to do this.

60

The Awful Truth About Business Cards

Michael Masterson has often pointed out in his online newsletter Early to Rise that much of the conventional wisdom you read about business and entrepreneurship is pure nonsense.

Much of this pap, as Michael has noted, is produced by misguided consultants, ignorant marketing advisors, and business journalists who have never run a successful business in their lives.

Take, for example, the nonsensical advice given on the subject of business cards.

One writer suggests giving everyone TWO business cards instead of one...the logic being the recipient will then have an extra to pass on.

Yet you never hear a Steve Jobs or Donald Trump say, "Yes, I built a billion dollar business...I used the 'hand out two cards instead of one strategy' to do it, too."

We're also told how to transform a business card from its conventional form (name, company, and contact information only) to a powerful "billboard" by adding unconventional elements such as a strong positioning statement, a list of services, or clever graphics or slogans.

But the truth is, spending any significant effort worrying or thinking about business cards...or strategizing their usage...is an absolute waste of time.

That's because most people who receive your business card throw it away without a second glance.

In fact, most of the self-made millionaires I know don't have business cards...or if they have them, they don't carry them.

In the "good old days," before the PC, most people actually had Rolodexes into which they would copy the information on your business card...or actually insert the card itself.

But now, your prospects keep their "Rolodexes" in Outlook or some other PC application.

Yes, I know there are devices sold that scan business cards and import them into PC databases. But their use is far from widespread.

Do you use one? Have you seen one on a prospect's desk lately?

That's what I thought.

So...what should you put on your business card...and how should you get it into people's hands so they pay attention and file it for future reference?

My answer may surprise you...

1. You shouldn't worry about what you put on your business card—it doesn't matter.

2. You shouldn't carry business cards or hand them out to people.

Instead, do the following...

When the prospect asks you, "Do you have a business card?" say:

"I don't have any on me. But give me yours, and I will put one of mine in the mail to you."

Then, in conversation, qualify the prospect, find out their needs, and send them the appropriate catalog, brochure, or other relevant literature on your products or services.

Enclose with these marketing materials one of your business cards—fulfilling the promise you made to send it.

But what if your prospect does not carry a business card (many busy people don't remember to carry them)?

Then have prospects write their contact information on a piece of paper (you should always carry a notepad and pen for this purpose).

You see, if you readily give your card to the prospect, you eliminate the need for them to give you their contact information...which means you have not captured a lead and have no way of following up with them.

But by strategically withholding a business card, you almost "force" the prospect to give you their contact information (almost no one will refuse you when you ask them for their card or to write down their contact information).

So you can capture them in your database...follow up to qualify them further...and convert those who are qualified leads to sales.

Result: instead of swapping little pieces of paper (business cards), you convert contacts into sales and revenues.

But there's one extra step I left out...

After you get the prospect's business card or contact information written on a piece of paper, say, "We also publish a monthly online newsletter on [TOPIC]. Would you like a free subscription?"

When they say "yes"...and most will...you can now communicate with them, virtually at no cost, as often as you like—both with your monthly online newsletter as well as e-mail marketing messages sent to your newsletter subscriber list.

You can send the e-mail marketing messages because, as subscribers, they have "opted in." They know you...have agreed to receive e-mail from you...and it's perfectly legal to send promotional e-mails to them.

Note: Of course, to use this strategy, you must actually publish an e-newsletter related to your product, service, or area of expertise.

61

One Thing Customers Really Want from You

Decades ago, my mentor, Milt Pierce, wrote what became a long-running control mailing for Good Housekeeping.

The envelope teaser: "144 Ways Good Housekeeping Can Save You Time and Money."

Why did this direct mail package remain unbeaten in the mail for over a quarter of a century?

Back then, saving time and money were two big appeals. And they remain so today.

In fact, in the 21st century, saving your customer time is more important than ever.

Why? Because your customers, like the Egyptian mummies, are "pressed for time."

We all have too much to do...and not enough time to do it.

One reason people are so busy is more working women: when both spouses work, there's no one at home to take care of all the household business...and so a working person has to do it.

What does this mean for you as a marketer?

Simply this...

In your sales and marketing efforts, if you can show the customer how you can save him time or serve him faster, your sales will skyrocket.

Conversely, wasting the customer's time is one of the surest ways to turn prospects off.

For example: in my little copywriting business I have a "virtual office"—my assistants work in their own homes many miles away from my office in River Vale, NJ.

Because of this, I work in complete isolation. So, some days, I break up the isolation by going out for a quick lunch to a local coffee shop.

While I was eating lunch a few weeks ago, at the busiest peak of the lunch hour, two young women walked in.

I immediately identified them as salespeople by the way they carried themselves, their manner, and their corporate attire.

Sure enough, instead of asking for a menu, they asked Peg, the waitress, if they could speak with the owner—who also happens to be the short-order cook.

Peg walked over to the grill and relayed the message to him. His irritation was immediate, visible, and audible.

In other words, he was pissed.

Peg came back and told the women, "I'm sorry, but it is the middle of lunch hour, and he is busy with orders."

Crestfallen, the two salespeople thanked Peg and left. Peg then turned to me, and said, "How stupid can they be—to call on a restaurant owner during lunch hour?"

Of course, she is right: by making a sales call during the height of lunch hour, these sales amateurs showed an utter disregard for the prospect's time.

He returned the favor by refusing to see them or buy what they were selling.

In contrast, here's an example of a company that won a big sale by making an extra effort to respect the customer's busy schedule and save him time.

Years ago, I did some work for a company—let's call them ABC Software—that was a software distributor to the corporate market.

A salesperson for ABC told me the following story...

He was trying to get a big corporate account—let's call them XYZ Corporation—to buy their software from ABC.

One of the advantages ABC offered was that they did not require a separate purchase order (PO) for each purchase.

The customer only had to issue a blanket PO one time to ABC to cover all purchases.

This saved purchasing departments a lot of time.

But even though ABC did not require a separate PO for each software package purchased, XYZ's accounting department did.

"My hands are tied," said XYZ's purchasing manager to ABC's salesman. "I'd like to use you, but I just don't have time to fill out all those POs."

"Not a problem," replied ABC Software's persistent salesman. "Just give me a stack of blank POs. Whenever you want to buy a software package, just let me know. I will fill out the PO for you, and then fax it to you for your signature."

By offering to lift the paperwork burden from the customer onto his shoulders, the salesman saved that customer a lot of time ...and as a result, won a major national account.

62

My Dad's Secret to Happiness

Writers and speakers know that you only have a few seconds to get the reader's or listener's attention.

If your opening fails to grab her, she'll quickly stop reading or listening.

One of the most attention-grabbing openings I ever heard was, unfortunately, that of the eulogy for my father, given at his funeral some 15 years ago.

"Everybody wants to be happy," the speaker began. "Dave Bly knew the secret of happiness, and in a few minutes, I'm going to tell you what it is."

Why was this lead so powerful? Three reasons...

First, it told the listener something she believed to be true: "everybody wants to be happy." And because it was true, it resonated with the listener.

Second, it promised a benefit: if you listened, the secret of happiness would be revealed to you within a few minutes.

And third, it was unexpected: not your typical dull eulogy.

So why am I telling you this?

Because the secret revealed that day was not only the secret to happiness...but, I realized, it was also the secret to creating winning marketing campaigns.

The eulogist didn't reveal the secret right up front, directly. He got to it through stories. I will do the same here, because it will make the secret clearer and teach it better.

The first story the speaker told was of a day when he and his wife, along with my father and my mother, went to a lake on a Sunday to enjoy the outdoors.

Three of them wanted to have brunch at a nice lakeside restaurant. But when they turned around, dad was out on the dock, talking to a couple of young boys who were fishing, but not having much luck.

Dad loved to fish, and he loved kids. Within a few minutes, he showed them his tricks for adjusting the bob, baiting the hook, and casting out...and they began catching fish after fish at a rapid rate.

The kids were delighted, smiling and laughing, thanking Dad for making their day. And he was smiling too.

The second story was about a little magic trick Dad would do to entertain when he went out to a dinner with a group of people.

When the wine was finished, he would ask one of the dinner guests to push the cork into the wine bottle, which they did.

Then he would challenge them to remove the cork—without breaking the bottle. Of course, they could not.

But Dad could—and did—to the entertainment and delight of the other diners.

(It's a trick that would take too much space to describe here. You do it with a linen napkin or handkerchief.)

"The secret of happiness that Dave Bly knew," the eulogist concluded, "is to put other people first. Make them happy, and you will be happy."

The same principle works in marketing and sales: make the customer successful...and help him achieve his goals...and you will be successful—because the customer will buy what you are selling, making you richer in the process.

So that's the simple secret of happiness...of marketing...of sales...and of success in virtually any aspect of life: put others first and you will reap the rewards.

And that's the secret I shared with over a hundred mourners at my father's funeral, when I gave his eulogy, so many years ago.

63

A Lesson from the World's Worst Salesman

Many years ago, Steve Martin made a short little film called "the world's worst waiter."

One site gag I remember was Martin as the waiter serving a turkey dinner.

The customer asks for gravy on his mashed potatoes.

Martin promptly turns his thumb down, sticks it into the gob of spuds, and pours gravy onto his shoulder; the gravy runs down the length of his arm and into the potatoes.

I was reminded of this by an outbound telemarketing call I received the other day by a financial planner who in my opinion, based on our brief call, would be a contender for the "world's worst salesman" title.

He explained to me that he was calling because I had responded to one of his firm's mailings and requested a free booklet on retirement planning–which I did and told him I remembered.

"Did you get the booklet?" he asked, reading the next question on his carefully crafted script–and in my opinion, a logical question to answer.

"No," I replied. "I don't think I got it."

Here's where he went off base.

"Well, it was sent over a week ago" he replied in a slightly confrontational tone, as if I had done something wrong.

"I didn't get it as far as I know," I explained patiently. "But I did request the booklet and would like to have it. Can you send it again?"

Obviously, he didn't want to send it again. He wanted an appointment to sell me financial products or services.

So instead of saying yes, he continued his confrontational manner: "Oh, I don't have it here," he said as if explaining logistics to an idiot. "Those are sent from the home office."

Then, instead of saying, "But I can call them and get one out to you right away," he followed with dead silence.

It was obvious my request for the booklet was an annoyance, interfering with his goal of getting an appointment. And he wanted to get my focus off this inconsequential matter.

"Well, if I can't get the booklet I requested, I guess we are done," I said. "Thanks for calling."

He literally stammered: "Well...uh...well ..." At that point, I thanked him again, told him I was really busy and couldn't waste more time with him, and since he wasn't going to help me get what I asked for—what his firm offered—we were done. And I hung up.

Listen: there are times when your objectives clash with the prospect's objectives.

Like in this case, I wanted the booklet I requested. He wanted to sell me something.

Well, guess what?

The customer doesn't care about you, your sales quota, your commission, or the mortgage payment you have to make this month.

He cares about himself, his desires, his wants, and his needs.

When you put the prospect's needs first, you win.

When you ignore the prospect's interests, wishes, and requests, you lose.

Now, some sales trainers teach that sending any kind of literature is a waste of time.

They tell you to say to the prospect: "I could send you a brochure, but that won't really explain our service. It would be much better for me to show you in person."

They say that because they believe their chances of closing the sale increase when they can get in front of the prospect.

But, if the prospect replies, "I want the brochure (or booklet, CD, white paper, or whatever you offered) first, and then I'll decide whether I am interested"–for goodness sake, give him what he is asking for!

Don't argue with him.

The "bait piece" strategy–offering free information to generate a lead–can easily double the response to your direct marketing campaigns.

But you negate its effectiveness...and actually make it work against you...if you either: (a) offer a worthless bait piece or (b) try to force the recipient into a sales situation without sending the material you offered.

One last example: I responded to an excellent radio commercial that offered a "free tape" on overcoming stress and anxiety.

But when I called the 800 number to get it, the inbound sales rep did everything in his power to convince me that I didn't want the free tape...but that instead I should get "the whole program"—a much bigger tape set costing hundreds of dollars.

I responded that I might indeed be interested in the program, and he could certainly send a brochure, but I wanted the free tape offered in the radio spot first—and that's why I was calling.

"Oh, you don't want that tape," he said. "That's just a longer commercial. It's really not worth listening to."

"If I don't want it and it's a worthless commercial, then why did you run a radio commercial encouraging me to send for it as a way to reduce stress and anxiety?" I countered.

In this e-mail, I've shown you the wrong way to use the bait piece strategy in direct marketing.

In my next e-mail (see chapter 65), I'll show you the right way to generate more leads and sales with legitimate, helpful "free information" offers.

64

Don't Lie to Me, Mr. Marketer

In my last e-mail, I told about the two worst mistakes you can make when offering "bait pieces"–free content–in your marketing as a bribe to prospects to generate inquiries:

(1) A ruse–offering something for free, and then telling prospects when they call, "Aw, you don't want that...buy my product instead."

I understand the sales strategy behind this inbound telemarketing technique: the marketer doesn't make money giving away free information. So the telemarketers are given scripts to convert as many inbound inquiries to sales as possible.

The problem is: they go too far. As I mentioned in my last column, I responded to a radio commercial offering a "valuable free tape" on how to reduce stress.

The inbound telemarketer tried to get me to order the full product on a 30-day trial basis. When I told him I wanted my free tape first, he said: "You don't want that. It's just an infomercial for the product."

Hey, if you offer me a "valuable free tape" ...and then tell me I "don't want that" when I call because "it's just an infomercial"...then guess what? You're a liar. And is that a good way to start off a relationship?

(2) Offering something that sounds like useful information, but when the prospects get the material, it is actually nothing more than promotional material, with little or no useful content.

Again, if you offer me a "free inventor's kit" as one radio advertiser does...and it's just your four-color sales brochure, with no how-to content on inventing...you're a liar.

Now, let me tell you about how to use the "free information" offer in your direct marketing correctly...so that prospects are satisfied with what they get...and feel good enough about it to take the next step with you.

Trillium Health Products used a toll-free number in infomercials selling juicing machines. The company's spokesperson, a juicing expert, appeared as a guest on a 20-minute segment of a radio show to talk about juicing.

Listeners were invited to phone for a free information booklet on juicing. The booklet contained juicing tips and recipes. But it also delivered a sales pitch for the machine.

That's important: the radio promotion promised useful, free content—and that's what prospects got.

But along with that, they got information on a product that they could use to implement the ideas and suggestions in their free report—in this case, juicing for health.

How well did it work? The radio show aired in a major market—Boston—and approximately 50,000 listeners called to request the free booklet.

Of those, 10 percent bought a juicing machine. So Trillium sold 5,000 juicers at $350 each for gross sales of $1.75 million—all from people who called a radio show to get a free booklet.

Another example: at the Hair Club for Men, founder Sy Sperling used a booklet called "The Consumer's Guide to Hair Replacement" as his bait piece.

It worked because the topic—a comparison of the hair replacement options available to consumers—was both educational and related to the Hair Club's product, a hair replacement system (hair weave).

The company generated thousands of leads every month—and closed enough to generate $60 million in annual sales—making Sy a rich man in the process.

One final tip: when you give away free information, make sure what you give away not only provides valuable free content, but also moves the prospect closer to a purchase.

"Once, we decided to give away a book on hair loss, instead of our own consumer's guide" says Sy. "This was a book published by a regular book publisher. The phone rang off the hook, and we thought the campaign was going to be a huge success.

"But we didn't convert many of those leads to sales. The campaign was a disaster and cost us a fortune.

"People were eager to get a free book just for the sake of getting a free book, but were not necessarily interested in hair replacement. The book, unlike our consumer's guide, did not sell Hair Club or our product enough to generate sufficient interest."

65

The Trouble with Competing on Price

A common strategy for small businesses is to undercut the competition by charging lower prices.

For instance, if every other graphic designer you know charges $100 an hour, you figure you'll steal business away from them by charging only $50 an hour.

Charging low prices...or "low-balling," as it is commonly known...is a terrible pricing strategy for service businesses—for several reasons.

First, your perception that a lower price makes you more attractive to clients is not universally true.

Yes, some clients are price buyers...and your low price will draw them in like moths attracted to a flame.

But there are many other clients who do not buy based on price.

These clients value other attributes—such as quality, reliability, speed, customer service, expertise, track record, and reputation—and are willing to pay a premium price to get them.

In fact, your low price signals to many of these buyers that you do NOT deliver those desirable attributes...and that you and your services are inferior.

The low price actually turns these prospects off!

This is not theory, by the way...

Direct marketers know that, in split tests of price, the low price for a product or service often loses and is less profitable than higher prices, which generate more orders and sales.

Low prices create a perception in the client's mind of low value.

As John Ruskin, the 19th century English critic, pointed out:

"There is hardly anything in the world that someone cannot make a little worse and sell a little cheaper, and the people who consider price alone are that person's lawful prey."

Second, your low price attracts a less desirable clientele–price buyers–than a premium price, which attracts clients who value good work and don't mind paying for it.

Price-buyers, while the least profitable clients to work for, are ironically often the most demanding and difficult to please.

Third, in a service business, time is money.

The less you charge, the less money you make–and the less profitable your business.

Given the choice, wouldn't you rather work for $100 an hour instead of $50 an hour...or earn $200,000 a year instead of $50,000 a year?

So, if low-balling is a bad pricing strategy, where should your pricing fall in relation to your competition?

Years ago, GD, a pricing expert, gave me the following rule of thumb for setting service fees: your price should fall in the middle of the top third.

So if the lower third of service firms in your trade charge $50 to $100 an hour...the middle range charges $100 to $150...and the highest-paid charge $150 to $200...GD thinks you should aim for $175 an hour.

Why?

Well, those in the lowest third are the low-ballers. They figure they'll get customers by offering "the lowest prices in town."

As we've seen, that's not a good pricing strategy for service providers.

The middle range isn't quite as bad. It can make you a decent living—and win you some good clients.

But if a low price creates a perception of low quality, a middle price can create a perception of mediocrity.

Is that how you want to be seen in your marketplace?

So given that, you should charge somewhere in the top third.

In the example given above, GD would say to charge $175 per hour.

I'm a little more flexible—and recommend between $150 and $175 per hour.

Why not go all the way and charge the highest price—$200 an hour?

Because at that price level, your fee becomes a huge concern to your clients.

It stretches their finances to the limit, and they begin to feel like you're trying to take them for every penny.

Also, almost all your competitors cost less than you.

By backing off the top of the price range a little, you can still command a premium price...but remove price as the foremost concern in the client's mind.

Bottom line: your price should be somewhere around the middle of the top third in your market.

66

Think Small

Over the years, I've met dozens of people who want to become speakers, consultants, coaches, TV or radio show hosts, or best-selling book authors.

Nine out of ten have told me the area in which they want to speak, write, or coach people is "leadership"... "success"..."motivation"...or some similarly broad topic.

These people are thinking big–pursuing broad areas where millions of potential readers, clients, and customers are seeking advice.

And I can virtually guarantee you that most of these wanna-be speakers, coaches, and gurus are going to fail miserably.

The problem is that they are thinking big–when they should be "thinking small."

What do I mean by "thinking small"?

"Micro-niching."

My colleague, speaker Wally Bock, defines a micro-niche as "the intersection of a skill or discipline with an industry."

So "customer service" is not a niche.

"Banking" is not a niche.

But "customer service skills for bank tellers" IS a micro-niche.

Why should you narrow the focus of your business—and target a small micro-niche—rather than offer a big idea, service, or product that everyone wants?

There are two reasons why micro-niching is a smart business strategy.

The first is competition.

If you want to position yourself as a "customer service guru," there's a lot of competition.

Everybody and his brother are trying to cash in on the need for customer service training.

And the barriers to entry are low.

On the other hand, if you want to become known as the customer service guru in the banking industry, there's a lot less competition—because it's a narrow niche.

The second reason why micro-niching is a good strategy is credibility.

If you proclaim yourself to be an expert in customer service, I'm going to be skeptical.

And more than likely, you'll have a difficult time proving your claim to me, your skeptical prospect.

Example: say you have worked as a bank teller for the last 11 years.

If you proclaim yourself to be an expert in customer service for the banking industry...and tell me that you have over a decade of experience in retail banking...well, you're instantly credible and believable.

Generalists are going the way of the dodo and the dinosaur. Customers want to deal with vendors who are perceived as experts in their field.

A few years ago, I opened the newspaper and saw that, in the Dear Abby column, a reader had written to express his disapproval of the way Abby had answered a particular question.

His letter began with the most wonderfully sarcastic line: "Dear Abby: How nice it must be to know everything about everything!"

Your customers are smart. They realize that no one can possibly know everything about everything, or even about most things.

The broader the areas of expertise you claim for yourself, the less believable you are.

By micro-niching, you become the "credible expert."

People believe you more readily...and want to do business with you because you're a specialist in exactly the service they need.

It's a win-win situation.

They get more accurate advice, better service, and confidence in you, their expert advisor.

You get more business, at higher fees, with clients who respect you and listen to what you tell them.

By the way, the narrower and more specialized your micro-niche, the higher the fees you will command—and the easier it will be to get leads and close sales.

For instance, offering your services as a "marketing consultant" is a tough field to break into, because so many people peddle marketing advice.

Positioning yourself as a "software marketing consultant" is a great micro-niche, except more and more people are doing it, and the field is getting crowded.

My friend Fred Gleeck positions himself as a marketing consultant for the self-storage industry.

There is little or no competition—and Fred owns most of that market.

After all, how many marketing advisors are interested in self-storage, or even know anything about marketing self-storage services?

Precious few, of course.

So the demand for self-storage marketing advice greatly outweighs the supply—and Fred can pretty much name his own price.

Now, maybe micro-niching won't bring you the fame of a Dr. Phil or a Dr. Ruth.

But other than that, what's not to like?

So take my advice—and find yourself a micro-niche today.

It will do your business good.

67

Don't Rush Your Bill

My single piece of advice for you today?

Don't rush your invoice to your client.

Your accountant and bookkeeper, of course, disagree with me.

"Get the bill out fast!" they urge you. "You'll get paid faster, and your cash flow will improve."

MB, the contractor who's been remodeling our bathrooms and kitchens for the past 6 months, certain agrees with them.

Every time I turn around, he's there with his hand out.

Typically, I get a call at the office during the middle of a busy day.

"I need the next payment," says MB, "can you have a check ready in 20 minutes when I stop by?"

Sure, I think to myself. I'll just stop writing, forget my own pressing deadlines, write out a check this instant, and sit here until MB gets here.

Yes, MB is entitled to get paid on time.

But on and off, I've been using him going on more than 20 years.

Certainly, I'm "good for it."

JL, who is MB's favorite electrician, also wants his money in a hurry, even if it's a small $100 repair job.

"I need this money today to pay my bills," JL will tell my wife—who of course immediately gives him the cash in her wallet.

The problem with being in a hurry to rush the next invoice—and get your money right away—is that it sends a message to your customer.

The message is: "I care more about getting paid than I do about your satisfaction or convenience."

I mean, come on: why can't MB send me a bill in the mail like everyone else, so I can forward it to my bookkeeper and let her pay it?

Recently, I hired a freelance writer to write an e-book for my small publishing company, CTC Publishing.

Today I got an e-mail with his first draft of the e-book attached.

Also attached to that same e-mail: his bill.

"Hey," I told him nicely. "I haven't even read your first draft yet. Why am I getting a bill?"

He should bill me only after he knows I am happy with his work...and not before.

Don't give your client the feeling that you're in a rush to send out an invoice and move on to the next job—even if you are.

The product or service your client ordered is what they want—and getting it makes them happy.

The bill is what they don't want...a negative to most people.

Therefore, so as not to destroy the feelings of happiness the buyer experiences when she takes delivery of the product she ordered, do *not* enclose the invoice when you deliver the product.

For instance, a consultant should e-mail his report as an attached file...wait a few days for the client to absorb it...and only then should he send the invoice.

Also, the client is in a rush to get your widget or report—but not necessarily to pay for it.

Therefore, it's desirable to send products and services ordered by rapid delivery methods—priority mail, FedEx, e-mail.

But the client is in no hurry to get your bill.

So don't e-mail it.

Dropping it into ordinary first-class mail is just fine for them—and for you.

Also, while it pays to be vigilant about accounts receivables, being overly so can tick off customers and rapidly destroy goodwill.

I pay my vendor invoices net 30 days unless I've agreed otherwise.

Yet I can't tell you how many times I have received a frantic call or e-mail from a proofreader, editor, writer, or Web designer demanding payment—for an invoice they sent me just a few days ago.

Not only is it annoying, but it again shows me their main concern in life is their pocketbook, not my satisfaction with what I bought from them.

"Don't rush a bill" is really just a specific application of a general, almost universal, business principle.

And that universal law of good business is simply: put the customer first.

68

Why I Don't Accept Referral Fees

For decades, I have made it a practice to refer my clients to vendors who can provide services those clients need...and that I don't offer myself.

I have also made it a policy never to accept a referral fee from any vendor, though many offer it, and some even argue with me when I turn it down.

I do not accept referral fees for this reason: my primary mission is to give my clients the best recommendations I can—and that means being totally objective.

It follows logically that I make recommendations that are the best for my client, not the most profitable for me.

And yes, sometimes what's good for the client is not good for the vendor.

For instance, I have many people calling who are eager to pay me thousands of dollars to write a promotion for them.

In many instances, I turn them down, advising that their idea won't work or their product won't fly.

By telling them this, I am saving them from financial disaster...but I am also talking myself out of a nice, fat copywriting fee.

Even worse, my recommendation that they not proceed is based on my nearly three decades of marketing experience.

Therefore, the advice is valuable to them...but I am not getting paid a dime for it, as they have not engaged me on a consulting basis.

I want my clients to know that the advice I give them is always in their best interest...and if I took referral fees from vendors, it would create a potential conflict.

I sincerely believe I would always recommend the best vendor for the job—not the vendor who paid me the highest commission.

But could I...or the client...be 100% certain I was always motivated by their best interests, and not a juicy referral fee?

The reason I bring this up is that PF, a copywriter, recently contacted me asking for referrals.

But unlike the many other coopywriters who want referrals from me, PF was offering me something in return—a free lobster.

Or rather, a $50 gift certificate to a Website selling Maine lobsters for each new client I referred to her.

Now, while I am against taking referral fees, I do make it a practice to send a small thank-you gift to people who refer business to me.

So if it's OK for me to send a small gift to a referral source, it seems like it should be OK for vendors to send small gifts to *me* when I am their referral source.

Now, I don't want them to do it. And I openly discourage it.

But, if a nice gift arrives in the mail, I usually don't send it back. I keep it and thank the vendor for it.

I don't think a small gift influences who gets my referrals—except, PF's free lobster offer sticks in my mind.

Actually, I don't eat lobster, which I know is unusual.

Any food that comes in its own armor is not for me...and truthfully, I don't even like the texture or taste.

But...

My oldest son Alex loves lobster...and a $50 lobster would put a smile on his face.

So when I am asked for a referral to a copywriter these days, by clients who can't afford my fees or to wait until I am available, I find PF's name popping up in my mind first.

Should you take—or give—referral fees from and to other vendors?

That's up to you.

But my position on this issue is: make your recommendations "pure," unbiased, and objective—and let your clients know it.

That way you get something far more valuable than the referral commission the vendor wants to pay you.

You get your client's trust—and a reputation in your industry as someone who is honest and trustworthy.

That's something—unlike a lobster—that money can't buy.

69

Be the One Who Wrote the Book On It

A few months ago, a VP at a local management consulting firm called me for advice on Internet marketing.

He wanted to start a line of information products related to the firm's consulting expertise; as I recall, it was something to do with meeting OSHA regulations.

"But I have to warn you, our president is dead set against the idea of creating info products on safety," he said.

When I asked why, he replied: "He is afraid it will erode our core business."

For this particular consulting firm, their core business is helping clients become compliant with OSHA regulations.

For their advice, they charge a handsome fee: $3,500 a day.

The VP worried that if he gave away their knowledge and expertise in relatively low-priced information products or even free white papers, potential clients wouldn't need the firm's expensive consulting.

Instead, they'd study the info products, do it themselves, and save a bundle.

I set him straight fast.

"Producing a line of info products won't erode your core business in the least," I explained.

"In fact, quite the opposite will take place.

"When people see you have published information products, they will—whether they buy your products or not—perceive you as a credible expert in the topic.

"This in turn will increase the demand for your consulting services, rather than cut into it."

Writing a book on your specialty—or publishing special reports, white papers, articles, CDs, DVDs, or other content—positions you as a leading expert in your topic.

You know the expression, "He wrote the book on it?" It implies that the person is an expert because he is the author of a book.

"It is simply amazing the reverence people have for the printed word," says EU, a successful publisher. "Simply because a person has written a book about a subject, people think he has something to say about it."

Selling information products actually widens the net of prospects who can benefit from your expertise.

It's difficult to get strangers to hire you out of the blue—after all, they don't know who you are, what you know, and what you can do for them.

But if you package your knowledge in a $15 paperback book, they'll risk spending $15 to sample it.

When they read the book, they will know that you know what you say you know—and believe you to be the expert you say you are.

So when you sell info products, you reach a broader—and bigger—audience.

What about the danger that the prospect will learn all your secrets by reading a $15 book, do it themselves, and deprive you of a big fat fee for your services?

That virtually never happens.

Instead, a qualified prospect reads your book and thinks: "The author really knows his stuff. But this seems complicated. I don't have time to learn it or do it myself. Instead, I'll just hire the author to do it for me."

Yes, there are probably other vendors the prospect could hire to provide the needed service.

But more than likely, you're the one they'll call.

After all, you wrote the book on it.

70

The Trouble With Cold Calling

I won't deny cold calling can work.

Yet in 99 out of 100 cases, I tell people who ask for my advice never to cold call.

The reason is that, even if the prospect on the other end of the phone expresses interest, the very fact that you cold called him puts you in a weak position—for three reasons.

First, people by and large want to deal with vendors who are busy and successful, not those who are desperate and need the work, right?

Well, when you cold call, your prospects assume that you are not busy and you need the work.

After all, if you were busy, you would not have time to sit there calling strangers and asking them for their business, right?

Second, cold calling puts you at a disadvantage when estimating prices and quoting fees.

A large part of what determines how much you can charge is the law of supply and demand.

When the demand for what you sell outweighs your supply, it's a seller's market and you can name your own price.

By cold calling, you are signaling to the prospect that the demand for your services is less than the supply—the amount of time you have available to render those services.

Therefore, prospects generated by cold calling are more price resistant—and more likely to haggle.

Third, cold-calling puts you in a weak position as you close the sale and negotiate terms with prospects.

Again, cold-called prospects know you want and need their business.

You are perceived as being easy to hire, and therefore prospects feel they can dictate deadlines, payment schedule, work arrangement, and other terms.

Why is cold calling so ineffective?

Because it violates the "Silver Rule of Marketing."

The Silver Rule is a universal principle of marketing and selling, first stated to me many years ago by my friend, marketing consultant Pete Silver.

The Silver Rule of Marketing states: "It is better for them to come to you, rather than for you to go to them"...where "them" is your potential clients.

You can see why the Silver Rule makes sense.

If you go to a potential customer, seek them out, ask for an audience, and plead with them to buy from you, you are seen as needy and desperate.

Your prospects think you can't be any good at what you do.

After all, if you were good, your book of business would be filled to overflowing—and you wouldn't be spending your valuable time on the phone, dialing for dollars.

The only prospects who buy from needy and desperate vendors are those looking for the low-priced bid.

So cold-calling risks doom you to being the low-priced provider.

When "they"–prospects–call you, instead of you calling them, the dynamic reverses.

They call because they have a need or problem...and because they are hoping you might be able to give them what they need or solve their problem.

But how do you get prospects to call you?

There are two methods. The first is good, and the second is better.

The first method is to generate inquiries through traditional marketing.

This includes Yellow Pages advertising...magazine ads... TV commercials... direct mail... radio spots...billboards.

When someone calls in response to your ad in their industry trade magazine, you know they have either an immediate need–or at least have some interest in what you are offering.

Otherwise, they would not have called you.

However, all they know about you is what they read in your advertisement.

Therefore, they may not be convinced that you are the right one to hire.

The second method of getting people to call you eliminates this problem.

This method is to establish yourself as a recognized expert or authority in your field.

You can do this through such activities as: writing articles or a column for your industry trade publication...

being interviewed as a guest on radio talk shows... writing a book (e.g., Tom Peters writes books on management)... giving speeches at industry meetings... writing a blog... distributing a podcast... publishing an informative print or online newsletter on your specialty... writing a white paper or special report.

When people call you because they read your book, they–like prospects who respond to your ad–are telling you that they have a definite or possible need.

However, the people who call after reading your book... unlike those who merely saw your ad... are already predisposed to buy from you.

After all, your prospects are skeptical of advertising claims.

But authors are perceived as experts.

You've heard the phrase, "We wrote the book on it."

When you are the one who wrote the book (or the article or column or content-rich Website) on the topic your prospects are interested in, you will be the one they call first when they need help solving problems in that area.

Action step: Think about how you can establish your reputation as a leading expert in your field or industry. Can you volunteer to be a speaker at the next big industry conference? Publish a white paper on your area of expertise? Write letters to the editor? Start a blog?

Best place to start: write an article about the solution to a big problem your prospects have and publish it in a magazine, periodical, or on a Website where they are likely to see it.

71

Get Smart

Years ago, a famous rock star–I recall it being either Madonna or Cyndi Lauper–returned to her high school to speak at an assembly.

Although she had not graduated, she told the kids: stay in school.

"The more you learn, the more you earn," she said.

Nowhere is this truer than in the business world.

Your success is likely to be directly proportional to the amount of knowledge you possess.

Knowledge about your products...technology... market...and your profession–i.e., copywriting, Website design, engineering.

Yet, even though we live in a knowledge-based economy, most of us graduate school knowing relatively little of what there is to know of the world–or even about our college major.

And with the dizzying pace at which new knowledge is created, the gap between what we know and what there is to know seems to grow exponentially with each passing day.

As Thomas Edison observed, "We don't know one millionth of one percent about anything."

Professor Richard Dawkins said in an interview with Scientific American magazine (7/07, p. 89): "All of us are ignorant of most of what there is to know."

So, with all of us knowing next to nothing ...what can we do to learn—and thereby earn—more?

First, find a niche—an area of specialization—and concentrate your efforts within that niche.

The narrower the area of your specialization, the better your chances of at least keeping reasonably up to date in the field.

Second, become an "information junkie."

Read constantly.

I recommend every person seeking success in some area of business read:

1. The leading trade magazines in their industry.
2. A daily newspaper.
3. A weekly news magazine such as Newsweek, Time, or U.S. News & World Report.
4. One or two of the top e-newsletters or blogs covering your area of interest.

Third, read *widely*.

Even though you are a specialist, you need to acquire a solid base of knowledge outside your field.

Of course, your time is limited, so even here, you must choose your course of study carefully.

So what should you read...and why?

MU, a PhD candidate and consultant in the science of innovation, says that to be more innovative and creative you must read in "adjacent areas."

An adjacent area is something different from but at least peripherally related to your major field.

Example: a systems analyst might read in architecture, because both deal with designing systems (the former a computer application, the latter a building).

Why do you need to read in adjacent areas?

Research shows that the ability to be innovative is dependent on possessing a wide storehouse of knowledge from which ideas can be generated.

People who are not well read have a limited store of knowledge, and therefore are hampered in their ability to come up with new solutions.

Of course, reading is not the only way to learn. Doing things is equally or in some cases even more valuable as a learning tool.

According to an article in Prevention magazine (10/07, p. 175), new experiences–doing new things–stimulates production of dopamine, a chemical involved in learning and memory.

In addition, new experiences build brain mass and increase mental agility, while the absence of novelty causes the brain to shrink.

Solution: take up a new language, hobby, sport, musical instrument, or any other activity that offers continual fresh challenges.

When does all this learning stop?

Never.

"School is never out for the pro" is old advice and still true today.

You might protest: "But I am too busy putting out fires at work for all this study and learning!"

Then do it after hours.

In his book "212: The Extra Degree," S.L. Parker advises:

"Add a few hours each month to your professional development outside of the work day."

By doing so, you can add the equivalent of a full week of work on your most valuable asset: you.

72

Choosing Your Signature Dish

In his reality TV show "Kitchen Nightmares," celebrity chef Gordon Ramsey rescues a different failing restaurant each week from the incompetence of its owner and staff.

One of his techniques for making restaurants successful is to help the restaurant create a "signature dish."

Of course, he does lots of other things, from revamping the menu and teaching the chef how to cook better, to training inept managers and cleaning up filthy kitchens.

But the signature dish—a single food item the restaurant becomes known for—is one of his favorite techniques for reviving a failing restaurant.

The signature dish, more often than not, is something simple.

For one restaurant it was a salad...another, a burger... a third, meatballs...a fourth, fresh made mozzarella.

In each case, the restaurant not only got back on its feet; it became known in the neighborhood for its signature dish.

So what does this have to do with your business?

In most industries today, there is more competition than ever: more companies competing with each other for business.

And in an age of choice, it's difficult to compete by being all things to all people.

A much better strategy is to specialize: in an industry, a product, a service, a method, a system, a task.

In other words, to have a "signature dish."

My colleague MS is a good example.

A very successful copywriter, MS can—and does—write many different kinds of copy for his clients.

But his specialty...his signature dish...is writing white papers.

Early on, he saw an opportunity for copywriting created by the huge volume of white papers being published.

He cleverly moved in to position himself as the preeminent white paper guru.

He did this by creating a separate Website on white papers.

He also published and gave away a free white paper on how to write white papers.

Today, MS has more business than he could ever hope to handle—writing white papers and other marketing materials for his hi-tech clients.

Now, many other copywriters...including yours truly...can write good white papers.

But all else being equal, wouldn't you rather go to the copywriter who is known as "the white paper guy"?

Of course.

Your prospects want to deal with experts—people whom they perceive as knowing what they are doing.

Since you can't know everything...nor is it credible to claim you do...the only way to be a credible expert is to specialize.

If you are a lawyer, you can specialize in forming offshore corporations.

If you are a dentist, you can specialize in sedation dentistry.

If you are a contractor, you can specialize in decks and sun porches.

How do you choose your specialty?

Here are some of the deciding factors:

>> What's in demand? What does the market need? What will they pay a premium price for?

>> What market niches are underserved? In what specialties is there a crying need for more vendors?

>> What education and knowledge do you possess or can you realistically acquire in a short time frame at reasonable cost and effort?

>> What niches do you already have experience and successful projects in?

>> What do you enjoy doing? What do you have an aptitude for? What skills do you possess? What are you best at?

One word of warning: don't pick a specialty you loathe or have no talent for simply because it looks lucrative or has little competition.

Remember the words of Aristotle who said: "Where your talents and the needs of the marketplace intersect, therein lies your vocation."

73

Your Fans: The 10-80-10 Rule

It used to bother me when I would get a bad review on Amazon for one of my books, or when one of my newsletter readers laced into me and criticized something I'd written.

But ultimate fighter Jon Jones has shown me that it shouldn't, because disdain from fans, reviewers, and buyers is just par for the course.

Jones, a UFC light heavyweight champion, uses the 10-80-10 rule for evaluating fan reaction to him.

According to the 10-80-10 rule:

**10% of the people out there won't like you no matter what you do.

**10% will follow you devotedly even if you don't deserve it.

**80% will swim with the tide. They can take you or leave you.

If you became a recognized guru in your field as a writer, publisher, marketer, speaker, consultant, coach, or expert you can expect to see the same pattern.

As wonderful as you think you are, most of the world—JJ says 80%, and I think that's about right—is indifferent to most of what you do.

It's not that you're not valuable, good, or important.

It's just that too many things are competing for their attention, and they don't have a lot of bandwidth left for paying attention to what you're up to.

You will discover a small minority, one out of ten according to Jones, who are rabid fans to a level that borders on irrationality; they just love everything you say, do, and produce.

Enjoy it, but don't read too much into it. You are not as good as they say and think you are.

On the other end of the bell curve, another 10% minority will almost loathe you and everything you say, do or write.

Human tendency is to strike back, refute, rebut, and retaliate.

I have done this, especially when some moron says something about marketing on a Linkedin group that I know to be wrong.

But I have to conclude that fighting against the anti-you crowd, as powerfully compelled as you may feel to do so, is mainly a waste of time and energy, energy that could be spent creating more stuff for the 10% of the world that loves what you do and the 80% that at times likes you.

When you ofer new products and services, aim that dead center at the 10% of the market who loves what you do. They will buy more of the new product or service than the other 90% combined.

The better you make your new product or service, the more copies you'll sell to the 80% of the bell curve who have some interest in your offerings but are not rabid fans.

Don't try to formulate products and offers targeted specifically at the 10% of the market that you just can't seem to get to like you. This is a waste of your time and they are not worth your time and attention.

Harsh, but true.

74

Why Groucho Marx and I Love Money

Subscriber LF writes: Bob, given your statements that you are not materialistic and shun luxury, what compels you to want to keep working so hard and making so much money? It seems as if by now you should have more than you need.

The reason why money is important to me has nothing to do with the things it lets you buy, because as LF correctly states, I don't want things.

No, the reason why money is important to me is the same reason why money was important to Groucho Marx.

Groucho said: Money frees you from doing things you dislike. Since I dislike doing nearly everything, money is handy.

In a nutshell, to me money equals freedom. In my case, the freedom to avoid doing things I do not want to do.

This point was dramatized the other day when, driving up to my home, I saw the grounds swarmed by a crew from the company that takes care of our lawn.

We have in the backyard more than an acre of woods, and all those trees produce a huge amount of leaves.

The day I pulled up I saw a crew of five men working with various equipment removing leaves from the property.

And I thought: If I had to do a job like that, I would want you to kill me.

You see, like Groucho, I dislike doing nearly everything, and I can't think of too many things more boring and mind-numbing than raking leaves.

When I drove up to my house that day and saw my lawn maintenance company at work, I felt like dropping to my knees and giving thanks that I make enough money to pay these five guys, whatever they cost, so I do not have to do it myself.

My definition of success for me, not for you, is doing what I want to do, when I want to do it, where and with whom I want to do it. And conversely, NOT doing things I do not want to do.

Very few things are as important to me in this life as avoiding tasks I consider menial, trivial, meaningless, tiresome, or distasteful, and leaf removal for me is in that category.

This belief system stemmed from spending my childhood watching my beloved father labor for decades at a job as an insurance agent that he hated.

I loved and admired my dad. But watching him make the ultimate sacrifice working as an insurance agent to take care of his family made avoiding a career that bored me or made me unhappy my top priority in life.

My main motivation in becoming a freelance writer was to be able to make money doing something that I loved; a joy that was denied to my father his whole life. I could not imagine having to do otherwise today.

Now, I don't make a king's ransom as a writer and I am not rich.

But, we are financially secure and comfortable, and the main advantage that our financial well-being gives me is the ability to, like Groucho, adamantly refuse to do the things I do not like to do.

Which is why I hire and pay others to take care of my lawn, repair my appliances, maintain my home, prepare my taxes, service my car, design my Websites, you name it.

My reward is the precious ability to do absolutely nothing but what I love, which is my work reading, thinking, and writing for my clients.

And that's why, yes LF, though while making and having a lot of money is important to me, I do not consider myself a money-grubber, even if you do.

Another misconception about money: Poor people think rich people are slaves to money—making, investing, and watching over it.

But money is much more of an issue for poor people than for rich people.

I have known and still know several people close to me who are financially strapped, and the truth is, when you do not have money, you think about not having enough money almost continually. They are living proof. (I could tell you stories.)

By comparison, having an ample financial cushion frees you from worrying and obsessing about money despite what some poor folks may think to the contrary.

75

The Truth about Content Marketing vs. Copywriting

GR, a freelance writer and marketing ignoramus, decided, in spite of her lack of knowledge, to deliver a mini-lecture on marketing writing on an online discussion group.

GR wrote:

"In today's market, stay away from advertising. Advertising doesn't work. Copywriting is finished. If you want to sell, you must write content, not advertising, Consumers respond to content. They hate advertising."

Here's the problem with GR's thinking in a nutshell: it isn't true.

Oh, don't get me wrong. Content marketing works. I know—I've been using it aggressively and almost continuously since 1980.

Content marketing has a lot of benefits. Mainly, it helps convince the prospect that you are an expert in your industry and that you know what you are talking about. And people like to buy from experts.

However...

Content is piss poor at closing sales and getting the order. And that's where copywriting shines.

The reason is that, at its lowest level, content is merely that—content. Information.

And you are not in business to write and give away free information. You are in business to make sales and profits.

Copy, by comparison, is deliberately constructed–using some very sophisticated techniques and formulas–to persuade a total stranger to give you money in exchange for your product or service.

One of those many formulas that copywriters master through long years of study and practice is the 5-step Motivating Sequence.

Content writers: have you heard of it? Can you name all 5 steps in the correct order? If not, I guarantee your writing does not sell nearly as well as it could.

Here is an article I wrote about it years ago for DM News: http://www.bly.com/newsite/Pages/DMNCOL35.htm

Why do many young writers sing the praises content marketing today while looking down on copywriting?

My theory–and yes, I know this is going to offend some of my readers big time–is that content marketing is EASIER than copywriting...by far.

When it comes to writing content–say, for instance, a good speech–there is a degree of skill and intelligence required, but not a lot of technique.

By comparison, writing a winning long-copy sales letter...one that raises conversion rates vs. the control by 25% to 50%...there is a huge amount of know-how, experience, and tricks of the trade needed to pull it off.

As a result, there are more content writers out there than you can shake a stick at.

While they vary in skill and quality, safe to say it's relatively easy to find a freelance writer who can churn out acceptable content.

Copywriters are another story...

Yes, there are also today, thanks to AWAI and others promoting copywriting as a business opportunity, more copywriters out there than you can shake a stick at.

But with copywriting, the number in the first tier ...those who write copy well enough to command top-dollar fees and repeat assignments from major league direct marketers...is a far smaller, select, and more manageable group.

On average, by my rough calculation, a good copywriter can earn 5 to 10 times higher annual wages than a good content writer.

There is a reason for this: great copy is a valuable commodity. It is rare than content writing and more valuable, with a much higher ROI.

4 Bonus Reports (a $116 Value)– Yours FREE

The essays in this book were originally published in my e-newsletter The Direct Response Letter.

You can get all my new essays for free without buying a thing by subscribing to my free e-newsletter now:

www.bly.com/reports

Subscribe now and you also get 4 free bonus reports totaling over 200 pages of actionable how-to marketing content:

** Free Special Report #1: Make $100,000 a Year Selling Information Online.

** Free Special Report #2: Secrets of Successful Business-to-Business Marketing.

** Free Special Report #3: How to Double Your Response Rates.

** Free Special Report #4: Online Marketing That Works.

Each report has a list price of $29; total value of this package of reports is $116.

But you can get all 4 reports FREE when you click on the link below now:

www.bly.com/reports

About the Author

BOB BLY is a freelance copywriter with more than 3 decades of experience in business-to-business and direct marketing. McGraw-Hill calls Bob Bly "America's top copywriter." Clients include IBM, the Conference Board, PSE&G, AT&T, Ott-Lite Technology, Intuit, ExecuNet, Boardoom, Medical Economics, Grumman, RCA, ITT Fluid Technology, and Praxair.

Bob has given presentations to numerous organizations including: National Speakers Association, American Seminar Leaders Association, American Society for Training and Development, U.S. Army, American Society of Journalists and Authors, Society for Technical Communications, Discover Card, Learning Annex, and New York University School of Continuing Education.

He is the author of 80 books including *Selling Your Services* (Henry Holt; over 50,000 sold) and *The Elements of Business Writing* (Alyn & Bacon; over 100,000 copies sold). Bob's articles have appeared in *Cosmopolitan, Writer's Digest, Successful Meetings, Amtrak Express, Direct,* and many other publications.

Bob writes a monthly column for *Target Marketing* magazine. *The Direct Response Letter*, Bob's monthly e-newsletter, has 65,000 subscribers.

Awards include a Gold Echo from the Direct Marketing Association, an IMMY from the Information Industry Association, two Southstar Awards, an American

Corporate Identity Award of Excellence, the Standard of Excellence award from the Web Marketing Association, and Copywriter of the Year from AWAI.

Bob is a member of the Specialized Information Publishers Association (SIPA) and the American Institute for Chemical Engineers (AIChE). He can be reached at:

Bob Bly
Copywriter
31 Cheyenne Drive
Montville, NJ 07045
Phone: 973-263-0562
Fax: 973-263-0613
E-mail: rwbly@bly.com
Web: www.bly.com

#

Made in the USA
Middletown, DE
13 September 2020